Enchanting Beijing

Memories of Beijing One Hundred Years Ago

京华万象

一百年前的北京

北京市文史研究馆 编
汪光华 绘 陈丁力 译

文化发展出版社
Cultural Development Press

·北京·

图书在版编目（CIP）数据

京华万象：一百年前的北京 / 北京市文史研究馆编．－－北京：文化发展出版社，2024.4
ISBN 978-7-5142-3873-0

Ⅰ．①京… Ⅱ．①北… Ⅲ．①北京－地方史－史料－1910-1920 Ⅳ．① K291

中国国家版本馆 CIP 数据核字（2023）第 047787 号

京华万象：一百年前的北京
Enchanting Beijing: Memories of Beijing One Hundred Years Ago

编　　者：北京市文史研究馆
绘　　者：汪光华
译　　者：陈丁力
封面题字：王世征
数字内容制作：中图云创智能科技（北京）有限公司

出 版 人：宋　娜
责任编辑：张雨嫣　　　　　特约编辑：范　炜
图书设计：观止堂_未　氓
责任校对：侯　娜　马　瑶　　责任印制：杨　骏
出版发行：文化发展出版社（北京市翠微路 2 号 邮编：100036）
发行电话：010-88275993　010-88275711
网　　址：www.wenhuafazhan.com
经　　销：全国新华书店
印　　刷：北京利丰雅高长城印刷有限公司

开　　本：889mm×1194mm　　1/20
字　　数：116 千字
印　　张：11
版　　次：2024 年 4 月第 1 版
印　　次：2024 年 4 月第 1 次印刷

定　　价：138.00 元
ＩＳＢＮ：978-7-5142-3873-0

◆ 如有印装质量问题，请与我社印制部联系　电话：010-88275720

编　委　会

主　编：李　昕　林丽颖　常晓霞
副主编：李明洪　邵　丹　宋　娜
执行编辑：刘卫东　徐小蕙　平晓东　赵　宇　杜　习
　　　　　邢聪敏　张雨嫣　张　璐　宿　欣　单　峰
　　　　　陈　曦　孙　明

EDITORIAL BOARD

Editors-in-Chief
Li Xin   Lin Liying   Chang Xiaoxia

Associate Editors
Li Minghong   Shao Dan   Song Na

Executive Editors
Liu Weidong   Xu Xiaohui   Ping Xiaodong   Zhao Yu
Du Xi   Xing Congmin   Zhang Yuyan   Zhang Lu
Su Xin   Shan Feng   Chen Xi   Sun Ming

PREFACE

A Panorama of Beijing in the Late Qing Dynasty and the Early Republic of China, a magnificent history painting depicting Beijing one hundred years ago, is the fruit of a yearslong project pulled together by Beijing Historical and Cultural Research Institute in cooperation with historians and Mr. Wang Guanghua, a famous overseas Chinese artist.

From a panoramic view of the ancient city undergoing dramatic changes, both the Inner and Outer Cities of Beijing (i.e., the walled city in Ming and Qing times) were in full display. The four edges of the painting consist of the Tonghui River to the east, the White Cloud Taoist Temple to the west, Yandun (a monolith structure) to the south, and the Juyongguan pass of the Great Wall along the Yan Mountains to the north. Readily discernible from this scroll painting are major historical events, activists and key figures, typical buildings, and folk customs ranging from the late Qing Dynasty to the early Republic of China. It has therefore been lauded as *Riverside Scene at the Qingming Festival* of Beijing in modern times.

During the early period of the Republic of China, Beijing was a city where cultures of either old and new, or east and west met. By combining the techniques of ruled-line painting and plain line drawing, typical of traditional Chinese styles of artistic presentation, Wang outlined the street and alley fabrics in detail, presenting to us the historical events swayed by the democratic ethos, such as the May Fourth Movement, the fire on Zhaojialou Lane, Chen Duxiu handing out leaflets at the New World Shopping Mall, together with folk customs, such as acrobatics busking, wedding and funeral ceremonies, etc.

Based on Wang's scroll painting, this book attempts to go into details of this masterwork by storytelling and take readers down memory lane to one hundred years ago for a panoramic vista of Beijing at the turn of the century. Meanwhile, it invites readers to immerse themselves in those century-old architectures still in service and have a closer look at Beijing's urban landscapes spanning over the past century with the help of the virtual reality technology. Aiming at bridging cultural differences and forging cultural identity through the fusion of history and reality, we hope this art book will enhance mutual learning between civilizations for readers around the world.

Beijing Historical and Cultural Research Institute

前言

《清末民初北京万象图》是一幅描绘百年前老北京历史风俗的画作,由北京市文史研究馆组织文史专家和书画家通力合作,历时数年精心创作而成。主创画家是知名华人画家汪光华。

这幅作品以全景视角俯瞰巨变中的古城,完整地展示了老北京内外城的全貌。画幅东携通惠河,西牵白云观,南起燕墩,北抵居庸关、燕山长城。图中描绘了从清末到民初在北京发生的重大历史事件、活跃的重要历史人物和典型的建筑、丰富的民俗风情,被誉为近现代北京的"清明上河图"。

民国初期的北京,新旧文化混杂,中西文化并立。画家将中国绘画传统中的界画手法和白描形式相结合,细腻勾勒城市肌理,将在近代民主思潮影响下发生的五四运动示威游行、火烧赵家楼、陈独秀新世界商场屋顶花园撒传单等历史事件以及天桥杂耍、婚丧嫁娶等市井生活汇集在一起,并一一加以呈现。

本绘本以《清末民初北京万象图》为蓝本,将巨幅画作中的细节加以展示,讲述画作背后的历史故事,以期带领读者走进百年前的北京,体会世纪之交的京华万象。同时,绘本辅以VR(虚拟现实)的沉浸式数字化技术手段,全景呈现百年建筑当下的发展变化,展现北京绵延百年的城市风貌,拉近不同文化语境下的文化距离,共叙历史与现实交融的时代文化认同,搭建不同国家之间、不同民族之间文明互鉴的桥梁。

北京市文史研究馆

目录

导　言	一百年前，世纪之交的北京	001
第一章	城市格局	004
	一、纵贯南北的中轴线	008
	二、气势恢宏的城门与城墙	026
	三、纵横交错的山脉水系	056
第二章	近代化进程	064
	一、盛景犹存的古都景观	068
	二、应时演变的近代机构	084
	三、极具风格的外国使馆	098
	四、逐渐兴起的近代交通	100
	五、接轨国际的城市设施	110
第三章	市民生活	122
	一、焕然一新的商业街区	126
	二、丰富多彩的市井民俗	142
	三、各具特色的宗教建筑	158

第四章　新文化传播　　　　　　　　　　　172

　　一、面向西方的教育转型　　　　　　　176
　　二、方兴未艾的公共活动　　　　　　　186

第五章　时局与事件　　　　　　　　　　192

　　一、清帝退位　　　　　　　　　　　　196
　　二、北洋兵变　　　　　　　　　　　　198
　　三、袁世凯就任临时大总统　　　　　　200
　　四、孙中山与袁世凯北京会面　　　　　202
　　五、国会风波　　　　　　　　　　　　204
　　六、黎元洪辞亲王匾　　　　　　　　　207
　　七、拆克林德碑　　　　　　　　　　　209
　　八、五四运动　　　　　　　　　　　　210
　　九、火烧赵家楼　　　　　　　　　　　212
　　十、陈独秀发表《北京市民宣言》　　　214

I

CONTENTS

INTRODUCTION
At the Turn of the Century: Beijing One Hundred Years Ago
000

Chapter 1.   City Layout   004

        The North-South Central Axis   008
        Lofty City Gates and Walls   026
        Crisscrossing Mountains and Rivers   056

Chapter 2.   The Modernization Process   064

        Magnificent Imperial Landscapes   068
        Evolving Modern Institutions   084
        Exotic Embassy Area   098
        Ascendant Modern Transportation   100
        Universal Urban Facilities   110

Chapter 3.   Life of Citizens   122

        Freshened Commercial Blocks   126
        Diversified Folk Customs   142
        Multireligious Sacred Architecture   158

Chapter 4. Spread of New Ideas 172

    Westernized Educational Transformation 176
    Dynamic Public Sphere 186

Chapter 5. Political Situation and Landmark Events 192

    The Abdication of the Qing Emperor 196
    The Mutiny Staged by Beiyang Warlords 198
    Yuan Shikai Assumed Presidency of the Republic of China 200
    The Meetings Between Sun Yat-sen and Yuan Shikai in Beijing 202
    The Turmoil in Congress 204
    Li Yuanhong's Refusal to Endowment 207
    The Demolition of the Ketteler Memorial 209
    The May Fourth Movement 210
    The Fire on Zhaojialou Lane 212
    Chen Duxiu and His *Manifesto of the Citizens of Peking* 214

At the Turn of the Century: Beijing One Hundred Years Ago

As the Eastward transmission of Western learning gained momentum towards the late Qing Dynasty, China was facing cultural shocks brought along by the Western civilization. Following the Westernization Movement, the Hundred Days Reform, and the invasion by the Eight-Power Allied Forces in 1900 completely shattered the pretentious ego of this ancient Oriental empire, expediting its reforming and modernizing attempts to save itself from both internal troubles and foreign attacks. Stuck in grave national crisis, Beijing, the last imperial capital of China, furthered its integration into the modern urban civilization.

Nothing could be done about the fatal destiny of the Qing authority, despite the reform which had been lingering through its final decade. But it did bring about elements of modernization in Beijing.

With the abolishment of the monarchy and the establishment of the Republic of China, imperial control over the city quickly faded away. Also abolished was the residential segregation between the Manchu imperial kinsmen and the civilians, which meant the once exclusively royal Inner City was to be open to the public. Together with the newly established modern industry and commerce, Beijing has embarked on a journey towards modernization.

As a series of municipal modernization projects kicked off, Beijing's landscapes have taken on modern forms. Supervised by the Beijing Municipal Office, the centuries-old Zhengyangmen Gate was transformatively rebuilt, avenues towards four directions were being paved, a pilot commercial block was under construction near Xiangchang Road of the Outer City, new buildings were being established from scratch, and municipal facilities such as roads, streetlights, and sewerages were being more widely applied.

一百年前，世纪之交的北京

　　清末，西学东渐之风日盛。古老的东方文明，日渐感受到西方工业文明带来的冲击。在洋务运动、百日维新后，1900年，世纪初的庚子一役彻底打破了古国帝王"天朝上国"的观念，清廷在内忧外患下被迫加快推行自救式的"新政"。北京，这座千年古都，进一步转入近现代城市文明的轨道。

　　持续十年的清末新政没有改写清政府败亡的命运，却为北京孕育出了城市近代化的萌芽。

　　帝制灭亡，中华民国成立，皇权的色彩在这座城市中迅速褪去。内外城的"旗民分居"格局被打破，曾经的皇城禁地面向公众开放，新政时期已初见端倪的近代工商业，使城市面貌发生了巨大变化，标志着北京正逐渐向近代城市过渡。

　　一系列新的市政工程开始启动，使北京的城市风貌带有更多的近代色彩。在近代市政管理机构京都市政公所的统筹规划下，矗立了数百年的正阳门被大刀阔斧地改建，东西南北几条大道即将贯通，新型模范市区在外城的香厂路开工，一幢幢新式建筑拔地而起，马路、街灯、排水系统等近代市政设施正被逐渐推广应用。

　　新式交通工具改变了人们的出行方式，铁路将全国各地的人带到了北京，穿梭在城市中的汽车、自行车和轨道交通，带人们领略这座逐渐融入近代化的城市的风貌。

　　市民的价值观念与风俗时尚的改变随之而来。帝都旧有的坛庙、御苑被改建为面向民众开放的新式公园，并相继建起了面向公众的博物馆和图书馆。

　　北京人口规模迅速扩张，随着不同社会群体聚集此地，形成了新旧文化杂陈

New means of transportation have changed the way people traveled. The railways brought passengers from all over the country to Beijing; people can explore a city freshly impacted by modernization via those bustling motor vehicles, bicycles, and rail transits.

What followed were changes in people's values and folk customs. While previous temples and gardens of the imperial capital were transformed into new parks open to the public, some of the city's earliest public museums and libraries were built one after another.

With the rapid expansion of population, Beijing has become the gathering place of various social groups and diversified cultures. The Legation Quarter was filled with expatriates and compradors, while traditional marketplaces such as Tianqiao and so on were buzzing as always. Booklovers patronized Liulichang, while pleasure-seekers found what they needed at Bada *hutong* (alleyways). New entertainment venues such as amusement parks, cinemas, ballrooms, photo studios, and billiard parlors provided new options in terms of people's daily pastimes.

The modern higher education of China also found its roots in Beijing. A batch of new schools, represented by Peking University, was established in Beijing, attracting and gathering a large number of intellectuals inspired by Western ideas. In parks and guild halls, they formed associations and gave speeches, constituting a new stratum attempting to voice for themselves.

With the development of the press industry, the propositions of political parties and elites have been transmitted to the public through newspapers, resulting in higher acceptance of the new culture by citizens and a much more open atmosphere. When Cai Yuanpei, the renowned educator, served as the president of Peking University in 1917, and when Chen Duxiu embarked on a critical trip to Beijing with the periodical *La Jeunesse*, the city was bracing itself for an intellectual brainstorm.

As part of the New Culture Movement, the May Fourth Movement broke out in Beijing in 1919. Young students took to the streets to shout out mounting concerns and fervent wishes for the fate of their own nation. When the wave of the movement spread across the whole country, it was time for the new revolutionary leadership to step up.

The 1910s saw the transformation of China's polity from feudalism to republicanism as well as her continuous exploration of the modernization process and incremental self-awareness. By playing a unique modeling role during the decade as the nation's political and cultural capital, Beijing can be seen as the window through which we observe China in that particular era: Where was it heading for, an either darker or brighter future?

的城市特质。东交民巷的使馆、银行尽是洋人与买办，传统的天桥集市依然是人声鼎沸；琉璃厂里的书籍飘着墨香，八大胡同中则是脂红粉白、歌舞升平。游艺场、电影院、跳舞场、照相馆、球房等新式娱乐场所如雨后春笋般地出现，让市民的日常娱乐活动也发生了新的变化。

中国近代高等教育发端于北京。以北京大学为代表的一批新式学堂在北京建立，吸引了大批受西方思想影响的新式知识分子在此聚集，他们在公园、会馆集会、结社、演讲，形成了新的知识群体，并开始发出自己的声音。

新闻报业得到发展，党派主张与精英言论通过报刊向社会传播，新的文化观念逐渐为市民所接受，北京社会风气日渐开放。当1917年，蔡元培出任北京大学校长，陈独秀携《新青年》杂志北上时，北京已经开始酝酿着一场思想上的大风暴。

1919年，随着新文化运动的不断发展，北京爆发了五四运动。青年学子们走上街头，用呐喊来表达他们对国家命运的关切。此后，这股浪潮席卷全国，新的革命领导力量最终登上了历史舞台。

1910—1920年，是中国从帝制走向共和的十年，也是中国在近代化进程中不断探索、不断觉醒的十年。这十年，北京作为全国的政治与文化中心，它的辐射、扩散、示范与倡导作用引领了时代的潮流。我们可以将北京作为一个缩影，来观察那个时代的中国，究竟走向何方？是在时代变革中沉沦，还是在逆境中崛起。

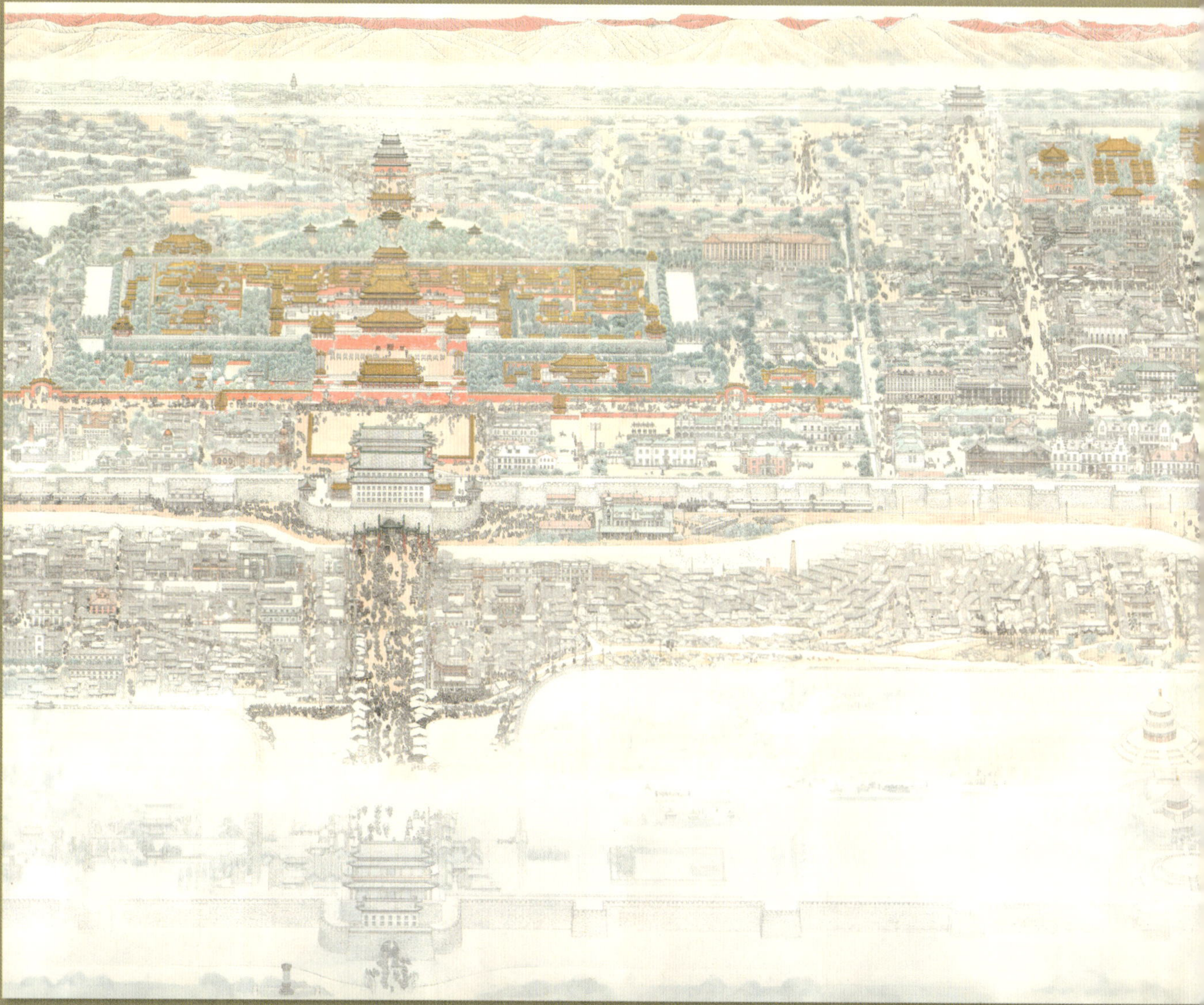

第一章 城市格局
CHAPTER 1 CITY LAYOUT

From the Yuan Dynasty onward, Beijing has been the capital of a unified Chinese nation. In order to manifest the supreme authority of the emperor as well as the hierarchical order of the feudal society, the city's planning and construction have been following the principles of having a temple on the left (east) side and an altar on the right (west) side, plus the palace in the front and the market in the back. Through additional construction during the Ming and Qing Dynasties, Beijing epitomized the best of Chinese ancient capitals.

Situated in the heart of Beijing as the emperors' residence, the Forbidden City was named after the Purple Forbidden Enclosure, the so-called palace of the Great Emperor of Heaven in Chinese astrology, for emperors in ancient China were believed to be the Son of Heaven. Reaching south as far as the Yongdigmen Gate, and north as far as the Bell and Drum Towers, the axis running through the Forbidden City resembles a meridian line on the ground, dividing Beijing into two parts that constitute a symmetrical and solemn city layout. The Capital City was molded like the Chinese character "凸" (*tu*, or like an inverted T), with the Imperial City, the Inner City, and the Outer City built from scratch surrounding the Forbidden City, establishing a quadruple-walled city framework. The closer to the latter, the more sense of imperial majesty it imposed.

Both the Capital City and the Forbidden City were surrounded by moats, and the city's water system was connected to the Beijing-Hangzhou Grand Canal by the Tonghui River. The Great Wall stretches for thousands of miles along the Yan Mountains just north of the capital, serving as a formidable barrier against military attacks from the north.

The introduction of Western learning in Beijing, the seat of government for the so-called Son of Heaven, resulted in it entering the process of modernization in the early 1900s. 1915 saw the reconstruction of Zhengyangmen Gate, one of the most vital projects of the ancient city walls. As they were knocked down by the wielding pickaxes, the city gates and walls have become the past memories of this imperial capital city.

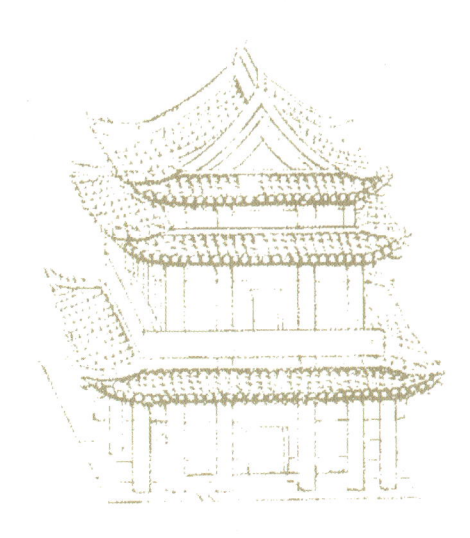

自元代始，北京就是大一统政权的首都。为了展现皇帝至高无上的权威和古代社会的等级秩序，整座城市按照"左祖右社、前朝后市"的形制修建。历经明、清的不断完善，北京成为中国传统都城的集大成者和辉煌代表。

紫禁城是天子居所，位于北京城中心。中国古代星象学认为紫微垣是宇宙中心，乃天帝居处，宫城命名为紫禁城，象征着皇帝的天子地位。以紫禁城为中心的中轴线，象征着大地之中的子午线，南起永定门，北至钟鼓楼，两侧建筑形成严谨的对称布局，彰显了对称之美。围绕着紫禁城，皇城、内城、外城拔地而起，整座都城呈"凸"字形，越靠近紫禁城，人们越能感受到帝王权力的威严。

护城河一层环绕帝都，又一层环绕紫禁城，形成了森严的封闭空间。通惠河连通着城内水系与京杭大运河，燕山山脉据守于京城正北，巍峨的长城在燕山上绵延千里，形成一道屏障，拱卫着京师，抵御着来自北方游牧部落的攻击。

20世纪初，当近代化的"西风"吹到这座古老的都城时，北京这座等级森严的天子之都开启了它的近代化历程。1915年，旧城墙迎来了最为重要的工程——正阳门改建工程。随着银镐的落下，一段帝都往事也永远留在了人们的记忆中。

纵贯南北的中轴线
THE NORTH-SOUTH CENTRAL AXIS

"A north-south central axis, spanning a length of nearly eight kilometers, runs through the entire city. It is the longest and most magnificent existing urban central axis in the world. The grand and orderly beauty unique to Beijing has been derived from the establishment of this Central Axis, and the city's undulating and symmetrical spatial layout has been based on it as well. The grandeur of this Central Axis lies in its longitudinal characteristic and consistent scale."

Liang Sicheng

　　一根长达八公里,全世界最长,也最伟大的南北中轴线穿过全城。北京独有的壮美秩序就由这条中轴的建立而产生;前后起伏、左右对称的体形或空间的分配都是以这中轴线为依据的;气魄之雄伟就在这个南北引伸、一贯到底的规模。

——梁思成

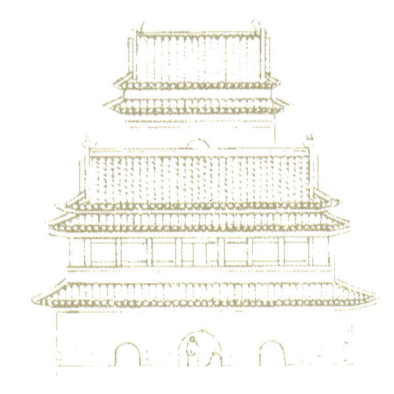

⊙ Yandun

On one's journey from the south to Yongdingmen Gate stands a 700-year-old monolith called Yandun. It was considered one of the five most superstitious objects in Beijing, believed to be capable of safeguarding the Capital City. Inscribed on its facades were two of the essays written by the Qing emperor Qianlong, both about the history of Beijing as a city and capital. According to the locals, this white marble monumental structure was one of the Eight Little Views of Yanjing (one of the ancient names for Beijing).

⊙ 燕墩

燕墩，位于进永定门的必经之路上，为京城五大"镇物"之一，距今已有七百余年历史，用以保佑京城平安。燕墩上刻有乾隆御笔亲撰亲题的《帝都篇》和《皇都篇》，是关于北京建都史的重要文献。"石幢燕墩"为民间流传的燕京小八景之一。

Zhengyangmen Gate (The Gate of the Zenith Sun)

The Gate of the Zenith Sun, more commonly known as "Qianmen"(meaning the front gate in Chinese), was not only the main southern entrance to the Inner City of Beijing during the Ming and Qing dynasties but also enjoyed the highest rank of hierarchy in architecture among all the other city gates. It had a rostrum at about 40 meters altitude, a barbican with four gates, a front bridge that was more elevated in the middle and lowered on both sides, therefore deemed as three bridges, and a five-bay archway (*pailou*). Located at the core of Beijing's Central Axis, it was a critical throughway between the Inner and the Outer Cities. The flourishing businesses and heavy traffic in areas outside (i.e., south of) the gate has formed the Qianmen Street still popular nowadays. Towards the late Qing Dynasty and the early Republic of China, modern city construction projects, including demolishing the barbican, retaining the gate tower and the archery tower, and opening a trans-meridional thoroughfare, were kicked off by the Beijing Municipal Office. Well-preserved among the others, the gate and its affiliated archery tower are both cultural sites protected at the national level.

Scan QR code for VR experience

正阳门

正阳门俗称"前门",是明清两朝北京内城的正南门,也是北京所有城门中规制最高的城门。民间素有"前门楼子九丈九,四门三桥五牌楼"的说法。正阳门地处北京中轴线核心区域,也是进出内外城的必经之路,所以正阳门外地区商业繁荣,车水马龙,形成了现在仍为人熟知的前门大街。清末民初,为了近代城市建设,京都市政公所开启了正阳门改造工程,拆除了瓮城,打通了东西交通线路,保留了城楼和箭楼。如今的正阳门城楼和箭楼是国家级文物保护单位,也是北京城内保存相对完整的古代城门。

扫码观看现在的正阳门

Yongdingmen Gate
(The Gate of Perpetual Stability)

Built along with the construction project of the Outer City during the Ming emperor Jiajing's reign, the Gate of Perpetual Stability was considered the southern starting point of Beijing's Central Axis. It was the main southern entrance to the Outer City during the Ming and Qing dynasties and the largest among the seven Outer City gates. It sat on the main traffic artery for those traveling to and fro China's Central Plain and the Capital City, therefore lots of stalls and teahouses could be found nearby where people would stop for food and rest. Towards the late Qing Dynasty and the early Republic of China, the hustle and bustle of rickshaws, carriages, wheelbarrows, and caravans on streets made such a lively scene.

Scan QR code for VR experience

永定门

永定门是北京中轴线的南起点，于明嘉靖年间加筑北京外城时（1552—1564）所建，是明清时期北京外城正南门，也是外城七座城门中形制规模最大的一座。永定门是中原进出京城的交通要道，城门内外有许多商铺、茶摊，供来往行人吃饭、歇脚。清末民初，这里黄包车、马车、独轮手推车、骆驼商队来来往往，一派热闹景象。

扫码观看现在的永定门

正陽門

⊙ The Structure of City Gates

The Inner City gates of Beijing usually consisted of six parts: the rostrum, the archery tower, the barbican, the gate tower, the stone bridge, and the archway. A passage linked to the main gateway was made bellow the gate tower. Usually, there was no gateway under the archery tower because of its defensive role. A stone bridge would be set up in front of each gate to facilitate moat-crossing. To the front of that bridge was an archway of a particular format (varied case by case).

Zhengyangmen Gate was superior to the rest because in addition to its main gateway under the rostrum, there was an exit under its archery tower as well as on both sides of the barbican. Above the moat was a wide bridge divided into three passages by railings. The middle passage stood right in front of the archery tower was exclusively preserved for the emperors according to ancient rituals, which means others could only use the two side passages. Its archway was divided by six columns into five bays.

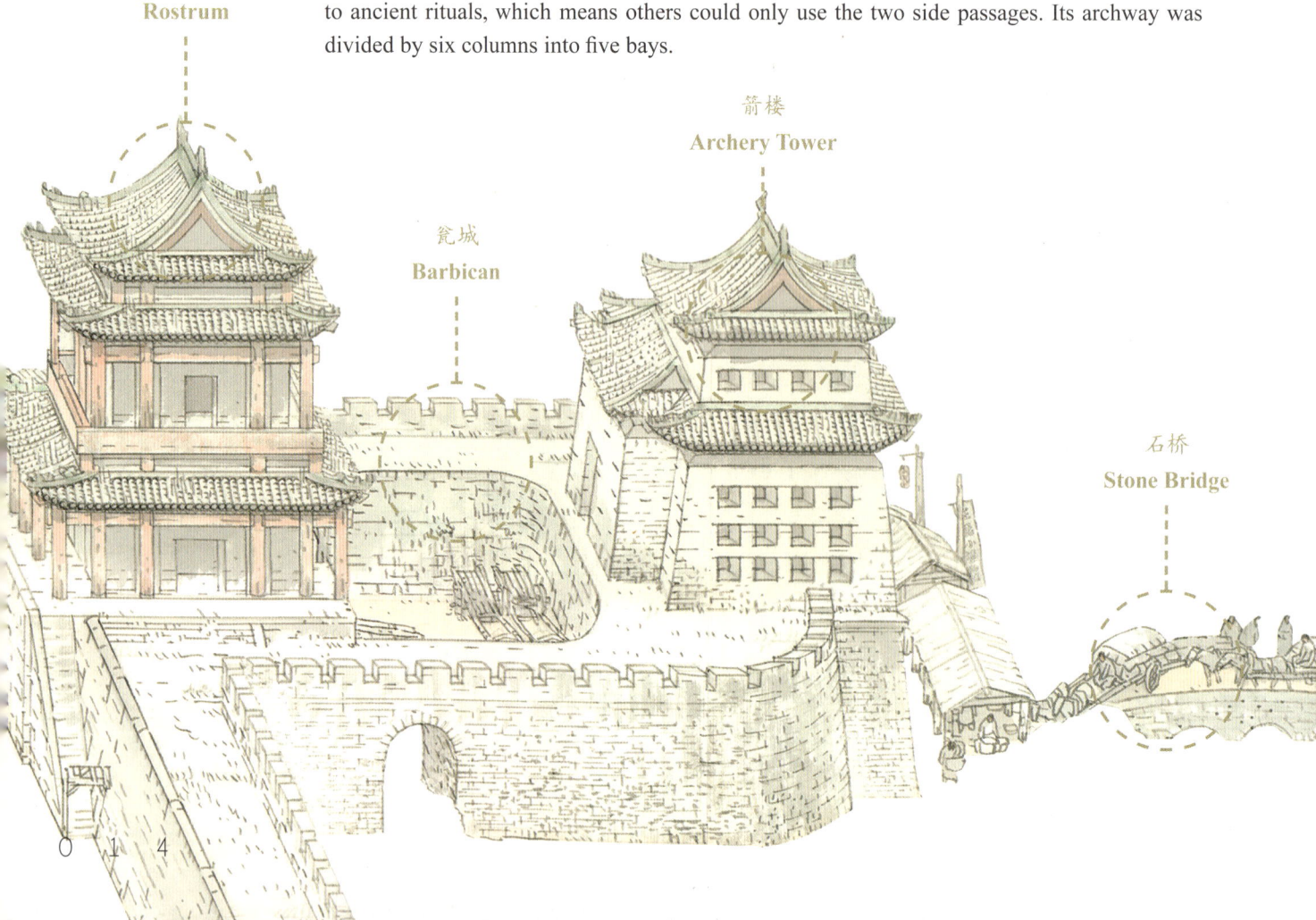

城楼
Rostrum

箭楼
Archery Tower

瓮城
Barbican

石桥
Stone Bridge

牌楼
Archway

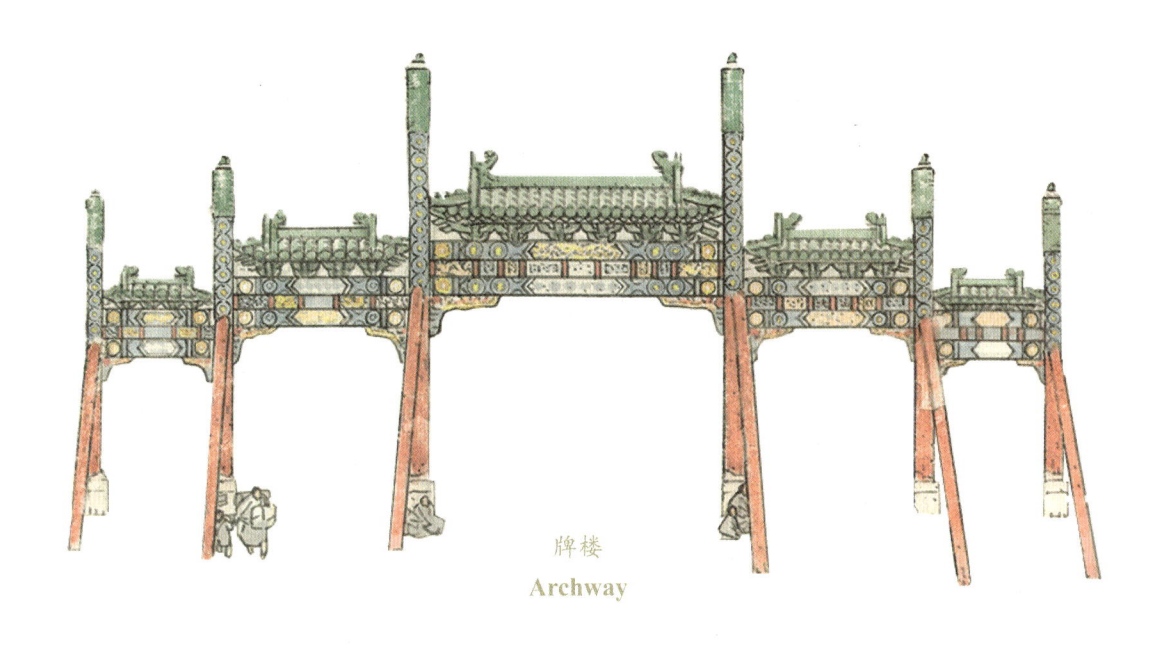

⊙ 城门结构

　　北京内城城门通常由城楼、箭楼、瓮城、闸楼、石桥、牌楼六部分组成。瓮城单侧闸楼下开一城门，联通闸门以供出入，箭楼则起到防御作用，其下并无门洞。由于护城河环绕，每个城门前都建有石桥，石桥前设置有不同规格的牌楼。

　　正阳门之所以规制最高，是因为除了正常的城门外，它的箭楼下也开有门洞，瓮城双侧都有可以进出的闸门。此外，护城河上的正阳桥十分宽阔，桥面被栏杆分隔成三条通道。按照古代的规制，居中的通道正对着箭楼门洞，称为御道，只有皇帝才能通行，其他人只能走两边的通道。而正阳桥牌楼的规格也是"六柱五间"，在所有城门中规格最高。这就是正阳门所谓的"四门三桥五牌楼"。

Tian'anmen
(The Gate of Heavenly Peace)

Tian'anmen is the due south gate of the Imperial City in the Ming and Qing dynasties. It consisted of two parts: the platform with archways and the rostrum. South of the gate stand a pair of *huabiao* (Chinese ornamental columns), seven outer Jinshui (Golden River) Bridges, and two giant pairs of white marble lions, one on each end of the bridges. Whenever there were big events such as the enthronement of an emperor, the crowning of a queen, or the dispatching of a general to war, grand ceremonies would be held on the rostrum. Among the five archways under the platform, the middle one which also stands right on the Central Axis is the biggest. No one was allowed to walk through except for the emperor of the day. Others could only use the side archways according to the ancient rituals.

During the Ming and Qing period, the area in front of Tian'anmen was an enclosed square held exclusively for the imperial families. Ordinary people were never allowed to enter it. After the abdication of the Qing emperor, the Beijing Municipal Office had a thoroughfare paved there, turning the place into a perfect location for public assemblies and processions. Events of historical significance took place here, such as the rally celebrating China's victory in World War I and the students' protest on May 4, 1919.

Scan QR code for VR experience

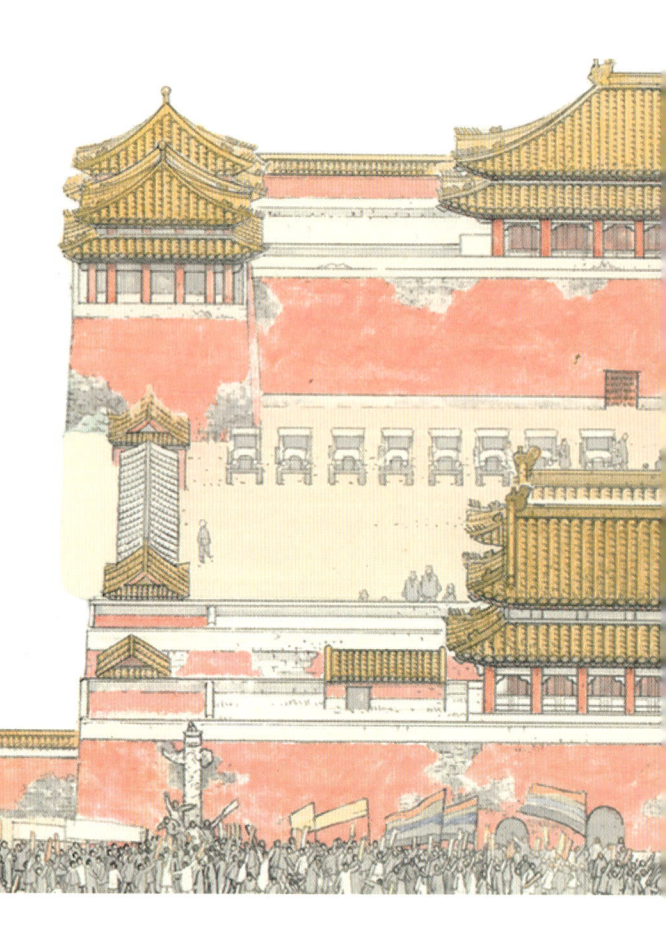

天安门

　　天安门是明清两代北京皇城的正南门，由城台和城楼两部分组成，门前有华表一对、外金水桥七座、桥内外各有石狮一对，凡遇皇帝登基、册立皇后、命将出征等重要事件都要在城楼上举行隆重仪式。城台下有五座券门，中间的券门最大，位于北京皇城中轴线上，在古代，按照规制，只有皇帝才可以由此出入，其他人只能走旁门。

　　明清时期，天安门前是一个封闭的宫廷广场，四周宫墙环闭，属皇家禁地，百姓不得进入。清帝退位后，天安门前的道路被市政打通，天安门前成了市民集会游行的场所。庆祝第一次世界大战胜利集会、五四运动时的示威游行等重要事件都在这里发生。

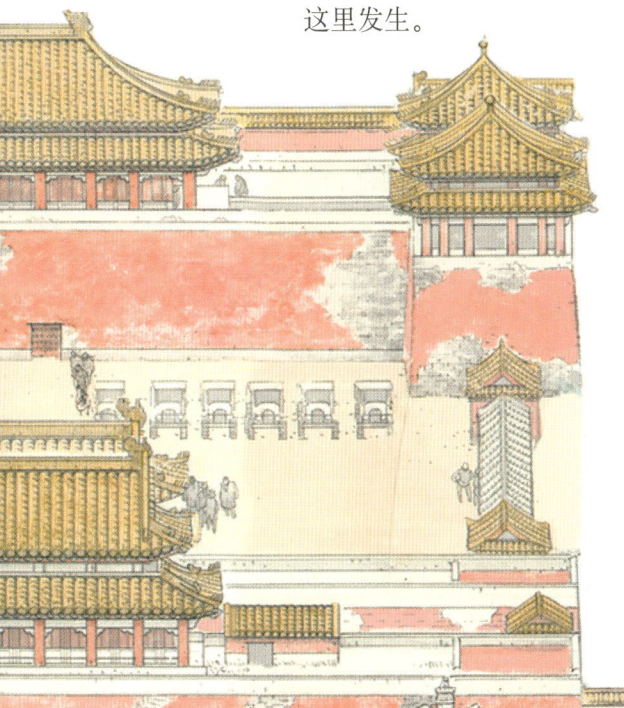

扫码观看现在的天安门

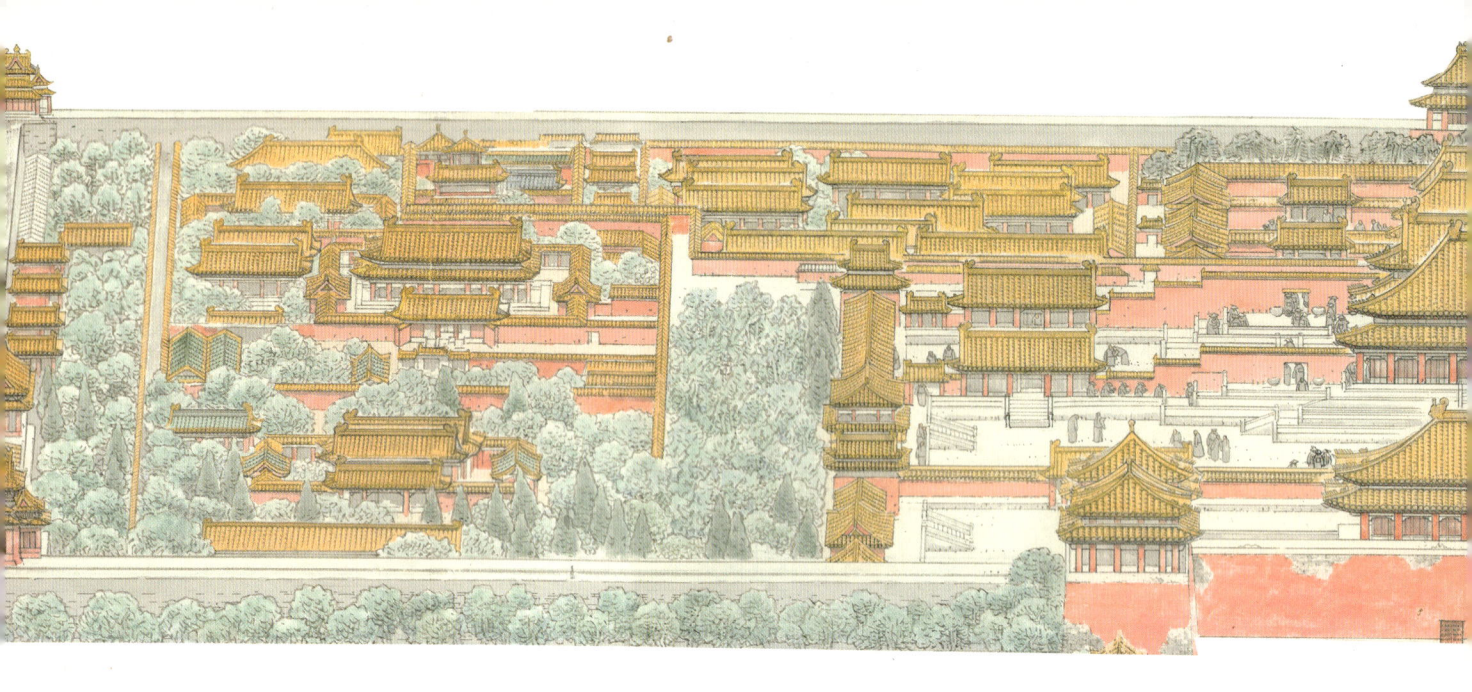

The Forbidden City

  Located at the core of the Central Axis and considered the heart of the city by being the royal palace of the Ming and Qing dynasties, the Forbidden City is well over 600 years old today. 720,000 square meters in size, it houses more than 9,000 compartments and is therefore the largest and best-preserved wooden palace complex in the world. As one of the world's top five spectacular palaces, the Forbidden City was home to 24 emperors in total.

  The Forbidden City was divided into the outer court in the south and the inner court in the north. Central to the outer court are the Hall of Supreme Harmony, the Hall of Central Harmony, and the Hall of Preserving Harmony, collectively known as the "Three Front Palaces", where the royal family held major ceremonies. Central to the inner court are the Palace of Heavenly Purity, the Hall of Union, and the Palace of Earthly Tranquility, collectively referred to as the "Three Back Palaces", where the emperor and his empress resided. The front and back palaces lined the Central Axis from south to north.

  On October 10th, 1925, the Forbidden City was renamed the Palace Museum. From then on, the public was allowed to visit this former imperial palace, which is seething with tourists all year round.

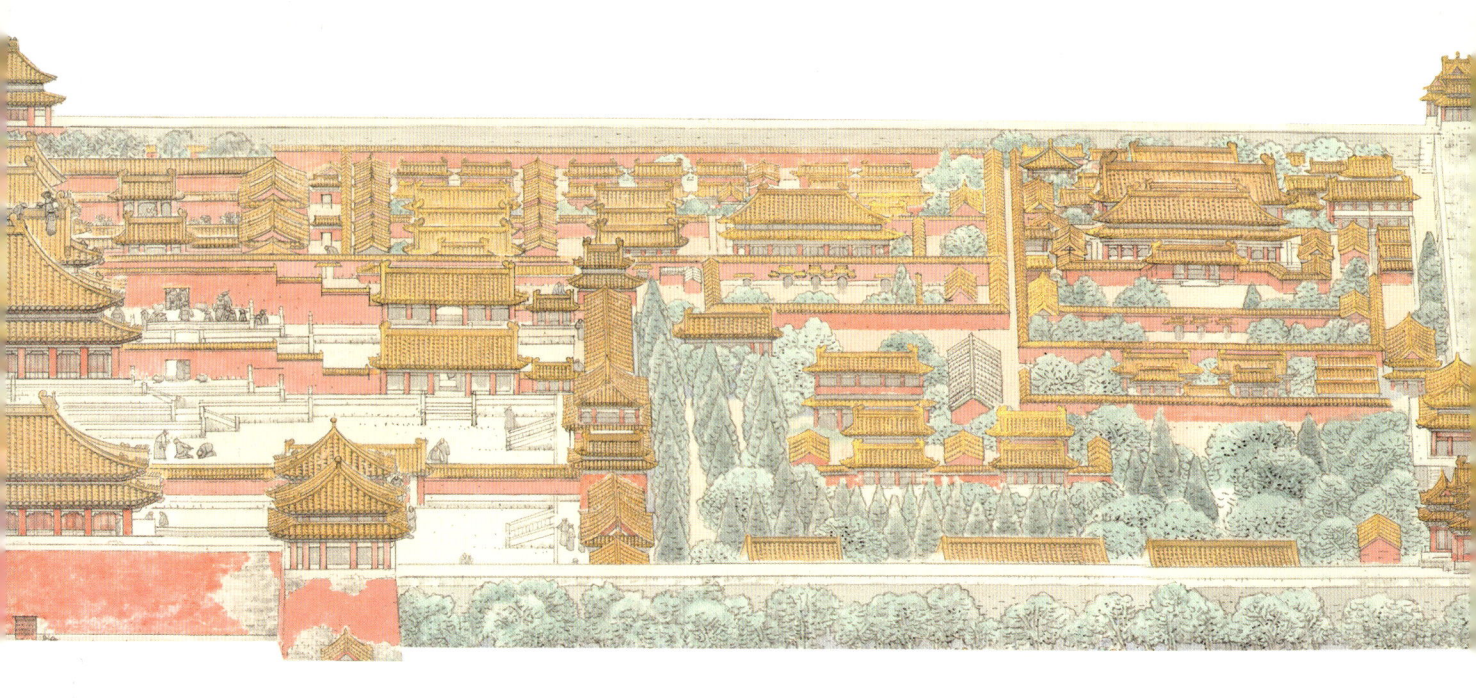

紫禁城

紫禁城是明清两代的皇家宫殿，位于北京中轴线的核心位置，也是北京城的中心所在，距今已有六百多年的历史。紫禁城占地七十二万平方米，房屋九千多间，是世界上现存规模最大、保存最为完整的木质结构古建筑群，也是"世界五大宫殿"之一。有二十四位皇帝曾经生活在这里。

紫禁城分为外朝和内廷两部分。外朝的中心为太和殿、中和殿、保和殿，统称"三大殿"，是皇家举行重大典礼的地方；内廷的中心是乾清宫、交泰殿、坤宁宫，统称"后三宫"，是皇帝和皇后居住的地方。三大殿与后三宫沿中轴线由南至北依次分布。

1925年10月10日，紫禁城正式更名"故宫博物院"，昔日的皇家禁地成了百姓皆可参观的社会机构，自开放之日起，游人便络绎不绝，直至如今。

Jingshan (The Prospect Hill)

Located outside the northernmost Shenwumen Gate (the Gate of Divine Prowess) of the Forbidden City, the Prospect Hill was an imperial garden during the Ming and Qing Dynasties. As the highest point in altitude in the Capital City, it was called Coal Hill or Longevity Hill in the Ming Dynasty and renamed the Prospect Hill during the Qing emperor Shunzhi's reign. Pavilions and terraces were added to the hill by successive emperors of the day, turning it into a prefect overlook at the Forbidden City. There were once the Hall of Imperial Longevity and other facilities alike at the site. In 1928, it became a public park.

Scan QR code for VR experience

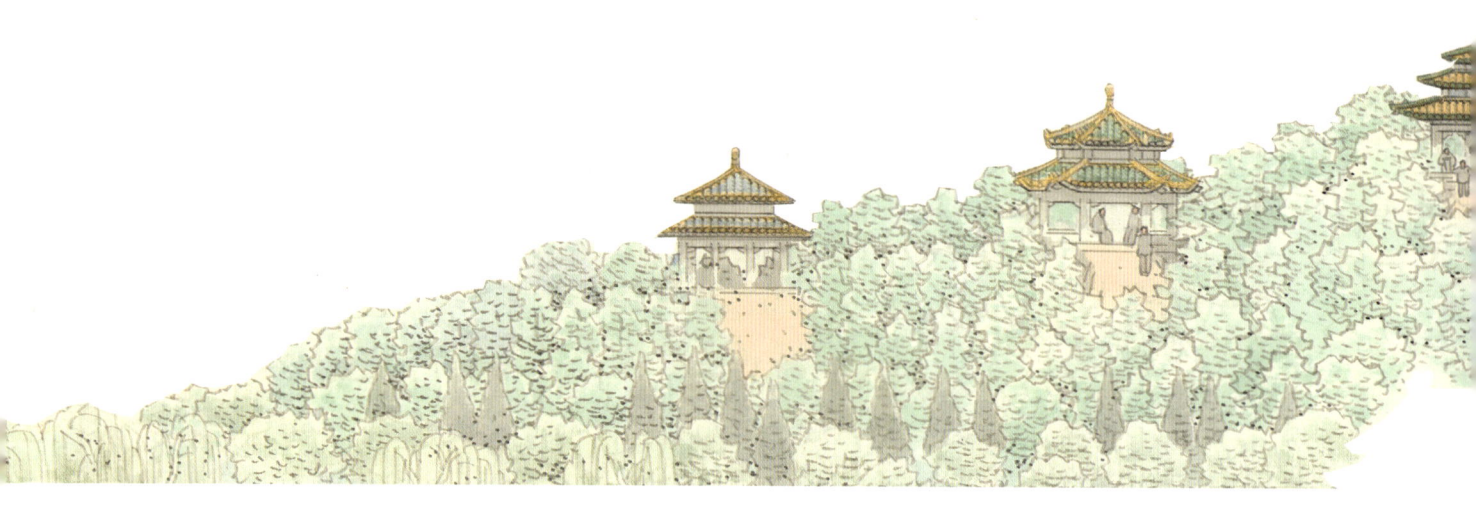

扫码观看现在的景山

景山

  景山位于紫禁城最北面的神武门外，是明清两代的皇家御园，在明代又曾称"煤山"、万岁山等，到清初顺治年间改称景山，是明清时期京城内的最高点。在此时期，帝王们陆续在山上修建有亭台楼阁，从山顶可以俯瞰紫禁城全景。此外，景山里面还曾建造有寿皇殿等。1928年，景山被辟为公园，开始对外开放。

Di'anmen (The Gate of Earthly Peace)

Opposite Tian'anmen in the south, the Gate of Earthly Peace is the northern gate of the Imperial City during the Ming and Qing dynasties. The couple symbolized peace in heaven and on earth as well as prayer for good weather. Built in 1420, the eighteenth year of the Ming emperor Yongle's reign, it was originally called the Northern Gate of Peace. In 1651, the Qing emperor Shunzhi gave it the name Earthly Peace. The gate was destroyed in a 1900 battle against the invasion of Beijing by the Eight-Power Allied Forces but quickly restored as it was the following year. The Imperial City walls to its east and west were dismantled in 1913 and 1923 respectively to make way for transportation. In late 1954, it was torn down for the purpose of easing urban traffic jams.

地安门

　　地安门是明清皇城的北门，与天安门南北对应，寓意天地平安、风调雨顺。地安门始建于明永乐十八年（1420），称北安门，清顺治八年（1651）改为地安门。1900年，地安门毁于八国联军入侵，次年按照原样复建。民国时期，为便利交通，1913年、1923年地安门东西两侧的皇城墙分两次被拆除。新中国成立后，1954年底，为了疏导城市交通，地安门被拆除。

The Bell and Drum Towers

The Bell and Drum Towers sit on the northern tip of the Central Axis, one on the south and the other on its north. Together, these twin towers constituted the time-telling center of Beijing from the Yuan to the Qing Dynasties.

First built in the Yuan Dynasty but demolished during the early Ming Dynasty, the Bell and Drum Towers were rebuilt after the Ming emperor Chengzu made Beijing the capital, since when they received numerous repairs. During his tenth year in reign in 1745, the Qing emperor Qianlong ordered the reconstruction of the Bell Tower which had been accidentally destroyed by fire before. As the site of public timepieces in the old days when clocks or watches were yet to be invented, these dual constructions played a crucial role in the daily lives of Beijinger citizens. The so-called "bell rings at dawn and drumbeats at dusk" reveals the mechanism of these time-telling tools. However, time service was no longer available here since 1924.

Scan QR code for VR experience

扫码观看现在的钟鼓楼

钟鼓楼

钟鼓楼是北京城中轴线的北端点，包含鼓楼、钟楼，两幢建筑南北纵置在中轴线上，是元、明、清三代北京城的报时中心。

钟鼓楼始建于元代，明初被拆毁。明成祖定都北京后，加以重建，此后多次得到修缮。钟楼曾不慎被焚毁，于乾隆十年（1745）重建。鼓楼与钟楼皆为报时装置，在没有钟表计时的古代，钟鼓声对于城市生活的正常运作发挥着极为重要的作用，人们常说"晨钟暮鼓"就是报时的体现。1924年，钟鼓楼最终停止了报时。

气势恢宏的城门与城墙
LOFTY CITY GATES AND WALLS

The layout of Beijing and its numerous city gates forms a quadruple-walled city framework, with the Forbidden City (with four entrances and civilian accesses denied) being its core and ripplingly surrounded by the Imperial City (with four entrances and civilian accesses denied), the Inner City (with nine entrances), and the Outer City (with seven entrances). There is an additional southern gate between Tian'anmen and Wumen (the Meridian Gate), called Duanmen (the Upright Gate).

Due to limited budgets as the construction progressed, the Outer City wall ended up unfinished with its upper half (i.e., the northern part) unbuilt, ensuing a city layout shaped like the Chinese character "凸", in which the walled square-shaped Inner City immediately north of the walled rectangular Outer City.

Imperial officials and ordinary people lived in the Inner and Outer Cities. The three front gates (namely, Xuanwumen, Zhengyangmen, and Chongwenmen) connecting the Inner City and the Outer City were the most prosperous area in the Ming and Qing Dynasties, where merchants and passengers gathered.

一直以来，北京城就有"内九外七皇城四"的说法，说的就是在重重城墙分隔下，北京城的城市格局与城门分布。

以皇家的宫城为核心，北京城由内至外排布着四重城墙，将北京划分为紫禁城、皇城、内城、外城四个部分。明代中叶修筑外城时，由于国力有限，外城仅修建了南半部分，所以北京城呈坐北朝南的"凸"字形结构。

每一重城墙均开有城门。紫禁城与皇城为皇家禁地，四面皆开一门以供出入，即皇城四门、宫城四门。另外，在皇城正南门天安门和宫城正南门午门之间，还有一座端门。

内城与外城为官员、百姓居住，由于人流量大，分别开有九门和七门。而内城的九门则是严格意义上的"京师九门"，其中连接内城与外城的宣武门、正阳门、崇文门的"前三门"一带，商贾云集、人流如织，是明清时期北京城内最为富庶之地。

The Inner City

Chongwenmen Gate (The Gate of Admiration of Literature)

  East of Zhengyangmen Gate was the Gate of Admiration of Literature, also known as Hademen Gate or Haidaimen Gate. The place was already a prosperous commercial hub during the Ming Dynasty thanks to the booming cargo ship business brought along by the Grand Canal. As the Outer City was completed during the Ming emperor Jiajing's reign, the gate emerged as a main road between the Inner and Outer Cities just as Zhengyangmen and Xuanwumen Gates, the other two southbound counterparts on the Outer City wall. Given its critical status as a business hub, a tax office was set up there. Since brewery was banned within the Inner City during the Qing Dynasty, spirits imported from outside the Capital City must be taxed as they were being transported through Chongwenmen Gate before being available for sales by the 18 officially designated distributors. No wonder the place was popularly known as the Gate of Alcohol or Taxation.

崇文门

  崇文门，位于正阳门东侧，又称"哈德门""海岱门"，自明代因为运河输送各种物资而成为商业繁盛之地。明嘉靖年间修建外城后，崇文门与正阳门、宣武门成为内外城来往的要道，并称"前三门"。基于崇文门为商品流通枢纽，明清两代均在此设有税关。清朝时，北京内城禁止酿酒，酒从外面运来，须经崇文门报税后，再交给清廷指定的十八家酒商统一出售，所以民间又称之为"酒门"或"税门"。

崇文门

Xuanwumen Gate (The Gate of Declaration of Power)

Paired with Chongwenmen Gate to its east, the Xuanwumen Gate was also called the Gate of Death because it was the route from the Inner City to the execution ground (known as Caishikou in Chinese) for prisoner transport vehicles in the past. There was said to be a warning remark inscribed upon the gate on its inner (northern) facade, which read: "It is too late to regret", as the death penalty was waiting ahead. Between 1920 and 1921, its archery tower was demolished to make way for the pavement of the loop line; in 1930, its barbican was torn down. After 1949, it was completely dismantled for the construction of a subway station of the same name.

宣武门

宣武门，与东侧的崇文门相对称。宣武门人称"死门"，因为门外就是菜市口刑场，囚车由此出入，犯人经刑部审核确定后，经宣武门押送出城，在菜市口问斩。据说，宣武门的城门洞顶上曾刻着三个大字"后悔迟"，意思是都到了这里了再后悔也来不及了。1920—1921年，为修建环城铁路宣武门箭楼被拆除，1930年又拆除了瓮城。新中国成立后，为修建北京地铁将宣武门彻底拆除，仅留下了地名。

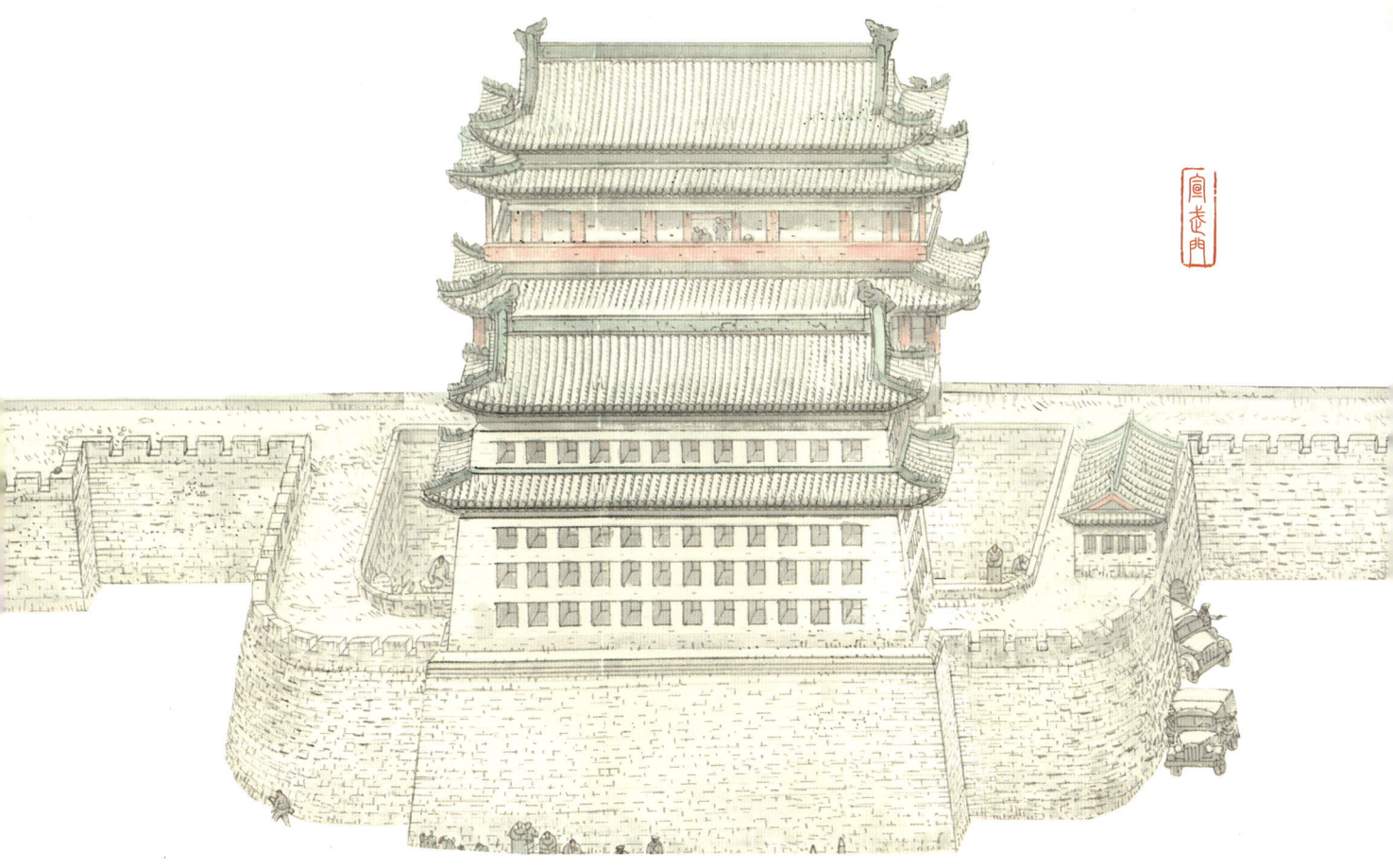

⊙ Caishikou

Caishikou has been a busy downtown of the Outer City. Every passenger from the southern provinces and heading for the Inner City would go by there after entering Guang'anmen Gate via the Lugou Bridge. Tan Sitong, one of the six martyrs of the failed Hundred Days Reform in 1898, let out his heroic last words before execution: "Though I have the will to kill enemies, it's already beyond my strength to reverse the defeat. What I've been pursuing is worth dying for, and I'm so glad I did it."

⊙ 菜市口

菜市口是外城的一处闹市，从南方各省来的人，过卢沟桥，进广安门，再进入北京内城，都要经过这里。戊戌六君子之一的谭嗣同被杀害前，曾在这里喊出了"有心杀贼，无力回天，死得其所，快哉快哉"的豪言壮语。

海运仓
Haiyuncang State Granary

Chaoyangmen Gate (The Gate of Facing the Sun)

    Formerly known as Qihuamen Gate in the Yuan Dynasty, the Chaoyangmen Gate was the southern gate on the east section of the Inner City wall. Before train was introduced to China, grains from China's southern provinces were shipped to Tongzhou via the Grand Canal before being transported to the granaries within the Inner City by land route via this gate, so it was also called the Gate of Grains and had a bunch of grain ears carved in the stone above the gateway. To the west of the gate were several state granaries—namely Haiyuncang, Beixincang, Nanxincang, and Lumicang—responsible for the provision of the Capital City.

朝阳门

朝阳门是内城东城墙南门,元代称齐化门,也俗称"粮门",专走粮车。因为那时没有铁路,南方的粮食需经大运河运抵通州,再经陆路由朝阳门运至城内粮仓,因此朝阳门的门洞内曾刻有谷穗一束。朝阳门内有海运仓、北新仓、南新仓、禄米仓等仓库,这些粮库担负着京城储藏粮食的重任。

⊙ The Russian Temple

During the Qing emperor Kangxi's reign, a Taoist temple west of the East Gate was assigned as the shelter for the Russian prisoners of war captured by China in the Battle of Yaksa. The Russians turned the temple into an Orthodox church more commonly called the Russian Temple by the locals. Later renamed the St. Nicholas Church, it was the earliest Orthodox church in Beijing and is now became the Russian Embassy in China.

⊙ 罗刹庙

清康熙年间，为安置中俄雅克萨之战中的俄军俘虏，康熙将东直门内一座道观划给他们居住。俄国人将道观改成了一座东正教教堂，民间俗呼为"罗刹庙"，后称圣尼古拉教堂，是北京的第一座东正教教堂。现在这里成为俄罗斯驻华大使馆。

Dongzhimen Gate (The East Gate)

Formerly known as Chongrenmen Gate in the Yuan Dynasty and said to be the earliest template for the other eight Inner City gates, Dongzhimen Gate was the northern gate on the east section of the Inner City wall. It was also known as the Timber Gate because, during the Qing Dynasty, most of the timbers from southern China were temporarily stockpiled east of the gate before they arrived at the Inner City.

东直门

东直门是内城东城墙北门,元代称崇仁门。相传,东直门是京师九门中第一座建造的城门楼,其他八座城门都是依据它的样式所建,故被称为"样楼"。清朝时南方运来的木材通常贮存在东直门外,京城里的木材大多都要从东直门运进城,所以又称"木门"。

Fuchengmen Gate (The Gate of Prosperity and Peace)

Formerly known as Pingzemen Gate in the Yuan Dynasty as well as the Gate of Coal, the Fuchengmen Gate was the southern main entrance into the Inner City from the western outskirts including today's Mentougou district, the coal-producing area west of Beijing. It was said that a bunch of wintersweet flowers was engraved upon the gateway because of the resemblance in sound between "wintersweet" and "coal" in Chinese, and in the fact that coal-burning brings warmth while wintersweets herald spring.

Since coal transport was quite heavy work due to the rough mountain roads, camels were frequently used to carry coal from the western suburbs to coal distributors scattered around the capital via the gate, where caravans coming and going had become a typical scene. In addition to their wholesale trade of briquets, those distributors also engaged in retail business through processing waste coal dust into lump coals by adding loess clay.

阜成门

阜成门是内城西城墙南门，元代称平则门，是京城连接西郊的重要通道，产自京西门头沟地区的煤炭都经由阜成门送至城内，故阜成门又称"煤门"。据说当时阜成门的门洞内还刻有一束梅花，因为"梅"和"煤"同音，老北京还有句俗话叫"阜成梅花报暖春"。

由于山路难行，加上驮煤吃力，骆驼成为运煤的主力，所以阜成门内外常见成群结队的骆驼进进出出，将煤运往京城各处的煤栈。煤栈除售卖批发来的成块煤炭外，还会将大量的散碎煤粉混入黄土，加工成煤饼、煤球后售卖给市民。

阜成門

Xizhimen Gate (The West Gate)

  Formerly known as Heyimen Gate in the Yuan Dynasty, the Xizhimen Gate was the northern gate on the western section of the Inner City, just the opposite of the Dongzhimen Gate, with a hierarchy in architecture rank second only to Zhengyangmen Gate among the other Inner City gates. During the Yuan Dynasty, the imperial family would only use water diverted from Yuquanshan (Jade Spring Hill) west of the city via this gate, therefrom forming the Jinshui River. In like manner, the domestic use of water also came through the sluice or the so-called Gaoliang River there. Widely known among locals was a naturally corrugated white marble inlaid upon the gateway of its barbican. The original site of the gate has now been replaced by a highway interchange of the same name, continuing to serve as a vital transportation hub.

西直门

　　西直门是内城西城墙北门,元代称和义门,与东直门遥遥相望,是京师九门中除正阳门外规模最大的一个城门。西直门又称"水门",在元代,当时皇家用水都是从玉泉山经由西直门引入宫城的,称"金水河"。而城市用水也是从西直门的水门引入的,称"高梁河"。在西直门瓮城门洞中,镶嵌了一块汉白玉,上面全是天然形成的水纹,所以有"西直水纹"这一说法。如今的西直门已被拆除,原址处架起了一座立交桥,仍是北京极为重要的交通枢纽。

Deshengmen Gate (The Gate of Victory)

Deshengmen Gate was located on the western section of the northern Inner City wall. The Gate had witnessed many historical events and was given the name the Military Gate. It was right here that the Ming statesman Yu Qian repulsed the invasion of the Oirats and safeguarded the city of Beijing. In this sense, the gate was one of the strategic passes to defend the city of Beijing.

⊙ Jishuitan

Within reach of the foot of the city wall near Deshengmen Gate was a watercourse called Jishuitan, which linked the moat with the water system of the Inner City. It channeled water from the Western Hills and Jade Spring Hill into the city, and was therefore looked on as the lifeline for the people living in Beijing.

积水潭
Jishuitan

德胜门

德胜门位于内城北城墙西侧，素有"军门"之称，也因此见证了许多历史大事。明代于谦抗击瓦剌部落侵袭的"北京保卫战"，就是在这里展开的。因此，德胜门是北京城最重要的城防阵地之一。

⊙积水潭

在德胜门城墙下方，有一水道——积水潭连接着护城河与城内水系，通过积水潭，城外西山和玉泉山的水才能源源不断地流入城内，可谓京城百姓的生命线。

Andingmen Gate (The Gate of Peace and Pacification)

Andingmen Gate was the eastern gate on the northern section of the Inner City wall. Returning triumphant armies would go by the gateway because its name signified peace and stability of the state. Indeed, there were nine gates on the Inner City wall but ten temples (two at Zhengyangmen Gate) inside the barbicans. Only those at the two northern gates, i.e., Andingmen and Deshengmen, were Taoist temples offering worship to the Taoist god Xuanwu (the Dark Warrior and Guardian of the North). The remaining seven were all Temples of Guan Yu (a famous general of the state of Shu Han during the Three Kingdoms period, and has been honored as a god of war and wealth by the Chinese). Emperors of the Ming and Qing dynasties would leave the city through the gate for the Temple of Earth offering worship to the Queen of the Earth every summer solstice to pray for bountiful harvest. In addition, carts carrying feces out of the city must go by the gate since there were middensteads fields on the east, south, and north sides of the Temple of Earth. Hence, the gate was jokingly called the Feces Gate.

安定门

安定门是北京内城北城墙的东侧城门,是出兵打胜仗后的凯旋之门,取"安邦定国"之意。京师九门有"九门十座庙"的说法,说的是内城九门的瓮城内都建有一座庙,唯有北墙上安定门和德胜门内建的是祭祀北方大神的真武庙,其他七门均为关帝庙,正阳门内还多了一座观音庙。明清两代,皇帝每年夏至都要经安定门到地坛祭祀后土,以求五谷丰登。另外,地坛东、南、北三面均有粪场,每天都会有粪车从安定门经过,故安定门也有"粪门"之称。

宣武门

The Outer City

You'anmen Gate (The Right Gate of Peace)

You'anmen Gate was one of the three entrances on the southern section of the Outer City wall, west of Yongdingmen Gate. Its gateway served as a transportation hub crucial to the southern part of the city. The area in the vicinity was actually the former towns of the Liao and Jin dynasties. Relatively remote from the downtown though, it was quite a vibrant place to live in, and traces of the capitals of previous dynasties were still visible. Besides, there were lots of ancient temples nearby, including Minzhong Temple of the Tang Dynasty and Sheng'an Temple of the Jin Dynasty. The gate does not exist anymore.

右安门

右安门是外城南城墙上的三门之一，位于永定门西侧，为北京城南地区的重要交通枢纽。右安门一带原是辽金故城，虽然地处偏远，但因延续了旧都的城市脉络，依然富有市井之气。附近古刹、寺院颇多，有始建于唐代的悯忠寺、建于金代的圣安寺等。如今，右安门已被拆除。

045

Zuo'anmen Gate (The Left Gate of Peace)

Located to the east of Yongdingmen Gate, Zuo'anmen Gate was one of the three entrances on the southern section of the Outer City wall. Functioning as the main route by land to Tianjin, Hebei, and Shandong provinces, the area was filled with hurrying passengers as well as diverse shops. Temples there were frequently visited by wealthy officials and literates. According to the the *Protocol of 1901*, an opening was cut through the city wall section between Zuo'anmen and Yongdingmen Gates by the British, enabling trains from Tianjin pulling directly in the station at Zhengyangmen Gate.

左安门

左安门是外城南墙上的三门之一,在永定门东侧。左安门作为通往天津、河北、山东等东南一带的陆路通道,每天行色匆匆的赶路人不在少数,因此这里也有不少店铺。左安门附近还有一些寺庙,常有城内官员富户、文人墨客前来游览。清末《辛丑条约》签订后,英国人在左安门与永定门的城墙上开了个豁口以修建铁路。自此,从天津来的火车直达正阳门下。

Guang'anmen Gate
(The Gate of Expansive Peace)

    Formerly known as Guangningmen Gate, the Gate of Expansive Peace was the only westward gate on the Outer City wall. It was one of the major entrances for passenger inflows into Beijing from the southern provinces, and once rebuilt according to the architectural hierarchy of Yongdingmen Gate, the main southern gate. Its marble-paved thoroughfare was definitely rare if not unseen at that time. Extended to as far as Wanping Town, the road made it all the more convenient for emperors' visits to the imperial mausoleums in Hebei province. That being the case, the area by the gate began to grow into one of the most prosperous parts of the Outer City where easy money was made. Towards the late Qing Dynasty and the early Republic of China, the place remained alive with lines of shops and restaurants.

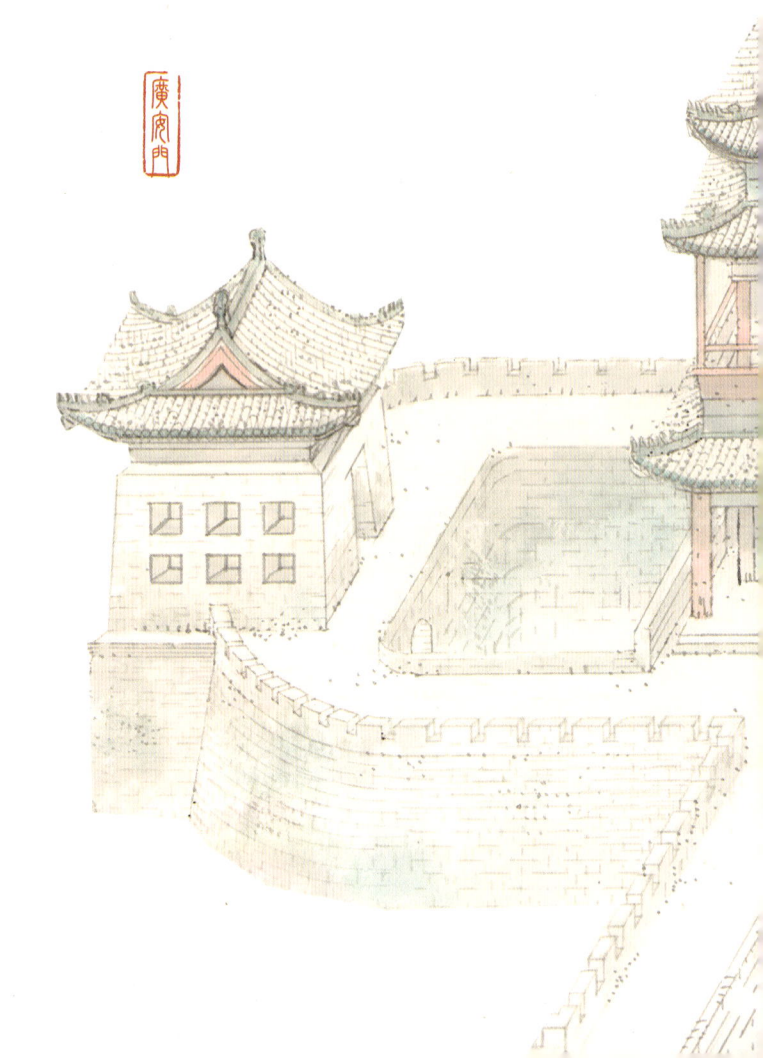

广安门

　　广安门是明清时期京城外城唯一向西开的城门,原称广宁门,是南方各省进京的主要通道之一,曾按外城正南门永定门的规制加以改建。当时,北京城铺设石板路的并不多,广安门大街就是其中之一。石板路由广安门延伸至宛平城,方便皇帝前往河北皇陵,也使广安门成为外城的繁华之地,流传有"一进彰仪门,银子碰倒人"的说法。清末民初,广安门依旧热闹非凡,各种商铺林立于此,各色吃食样样俱全。

⊙ The Tomb of Yuan Chonghuan

As a celebrated general of the late Ming Dynasty, Yuan Chonghuan was buried somewhere west of Guangqumen Gate, where people would pay tribute to during the late Qing and early Republic of China periods.

⊙ 袁崇焕墓

明末著名将领袁崇焕就葬在广渠门内，直至清末民初还会有百姓到其墓前祭奠。

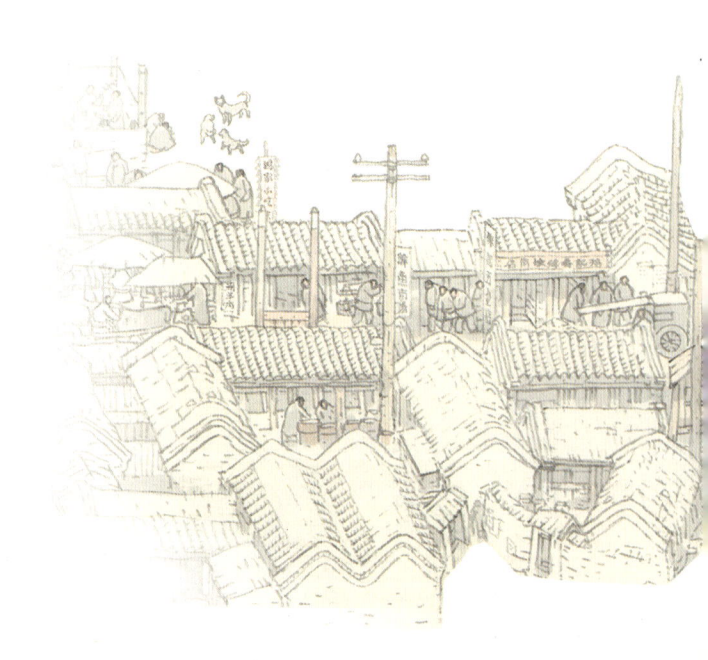

Guangqumen Gate

Commonly known as Shawomen Gate, Guangqumen Gate was the only eastward gate on the Outer City wall. This gateway was considered a relatively vulnerable spot in the defense system of the Capital City. Yuan Chonghuan, a military leader in the late Ming Dynasty, repelled the assaulting Qing soldiers outside the gate with a cavalry regiment of merely 9,000 soldiers. However, he was executed by emperor Chongzhen because of dissension and alienation, which eventually led to the fall of Ming. After occupying Tianjin in 1900, the Eight-Power Allied Forces attempted to invade Beijing via this sally port. It witnessed two major campaigns as well as the decline of two feudal dynasties.

广渠门

　　广渠门,又称沙窝门,是明清北京外城唯一向东开的城门。广渠门是京城防御较为薄弱的地方。明末将领袁崇焕曾率领九千骑兵在广渠门外击退清朝军队,却因反间计被崇祯皇帝处死,最终直接导致明朝灭亡。1900年,八国联军占领天津后,也从守备较弱的广渠门打开缺口进入北京。可以说广渠门经历了明末和清末的两次大战,也见证了两个朝代走向终结。

Dongbianmen Gate
(The East Side Gate)

  The Dongbianmen Gate was on the eastern section of the northern Outer City wall. When the Ming emperor Jiajing had the Outer City wall built at the outset, he did not expect the budget would be too tight to complete the project as it was planned. Subsequently, a makeshift plan was figured out that the eastern Outer City wall took a westward turn until it ended up at the southeast corner tower of the Inner City wall, and vice versa. Both the East and West Side Gates were opened on the northern section of the Outer City wall as shortcuts. Outside the gate there was one a waterside area, the confluence of the moats from the Inner and Outer Cities. Freight terminals there were bustling with water transport. The charming scenery such as boats in the rippling moat under the weeping willows made it a perfect hiking spot for locals.

东便门

　　东便门是北京外城北城墙东段上的城门。嘉靖年间修筑外城时，由于财力不济，朝廷最终决定将从南面修筑的外城城墙包筑于内城东南角楼和西南角楼北侧。东、西两座便门便开在面北的外城城墙上，以方便人们进出。东便门外素有"水乡"之称。这里是内城和外城两条护城河的交汇处，漕运码头货运繁忙，护城河上舟楫往来，清风拂柳，碧波荡漾，是京城人踏青郊游的佳处。

054

Xibianmen Gate (The West Side Gate)

The Xibianmen Gate was on the western section of the northern Outer City wall. Its appearance was the lowest in architectural hierarchy compared to the remaining six counterparts. This was the must way for people within range of that part of the Outer City heading for a northwest-bound journey. Outside the gate, there was once a patch of green so picturesque that the landscapes there had once become one of the many alternatives for Ten Sights of Yanjing, referred to as the flock of sheep at Xibianmen Gate. The grass north of the gate was scattered with a dozen white stones, which, when viewed from a distance, could be mistaken for a tranquil flock of grazing sheep.

西便门

西便门是北京外城北城墙西段上的城门，是外城七门中规模最小的一个。西便门是外城出城向西北方向走的孔道，门外水草丰茂。民间流传的又一版本的"燕京十景"中有"西便群羊"一景，就是指西便门外草地中散落的数十块形状不一的白石头，远远望去就像白色的羊群在草地上悠闲吃草。

纵横交错的山脉水系

CRISSCROSSING MOUNTAINS AND RIVERS

The Water System from the Jade Spring Hill

Located west of Beijing, Jade Spring Hill is known for its rocky hills, secluded caves, babbling streams, and gurgling spring water. From the Yuan to the Qing dynasties, drinking water consumed by the imperial palace was drawn from these springs. The source of the spring was initially heading east for Qinghe River until a rechanneling project resulted in its southeastward diversion into Kunming Lake before it ran down along the Changhe (Long River) into Jishuitan, where it split into two southward branches and later formed the Six Lake. They eventually went through the Dongbianmen Gate and fluxed into the Tonghui River.

⊙ The Six Lakes of Beijing

The Six Lakes collectively refers to a vital water system comprised of lakes in downtown Beijing. The three lakes of Shichahai are known as Xihai (West Lake), Houhai (Back Lake), and Qianhai (Front Lake). The other three on their south are known as Beihai (North Lake), Zhonghai (Central Lake), and Nanhai (South Lake). Originally a natural wetland and of the water veins of the Gaoliang River system, the Six Lakes gradually converged with the water system from the Jade Spring Hill and became the lifeline of Beijing's water system through natural changes and historical transformation.

玉泉山水系

玉泉山位于北京城西郊，其间奇岩幽洞，小溪潺潺，流泉活水。元明清三代，宫廷的饮用水皆为玉泉之水。玉泉山的水原本向东流入清河，后经改造，向东南注入昆明湖，再从长河进入北京城内积水潭，随后分两路继续南流，汇入城内的前、后三海，最后向东由东便门流入通惠河。

⊙ 北京"六海"

北京"六海"是指西海、后海、前海（即今什刹三海，又称"后三海"）、北海、中海和南海（合称"前三海"）的一片水域，是北京城内的重要水系。这里本是一片天然河湖湿地，是高粱河水系的水脉，历经自然变化与历代改造，并汇入玉泉山水系，成为北京城市水系的主脉。

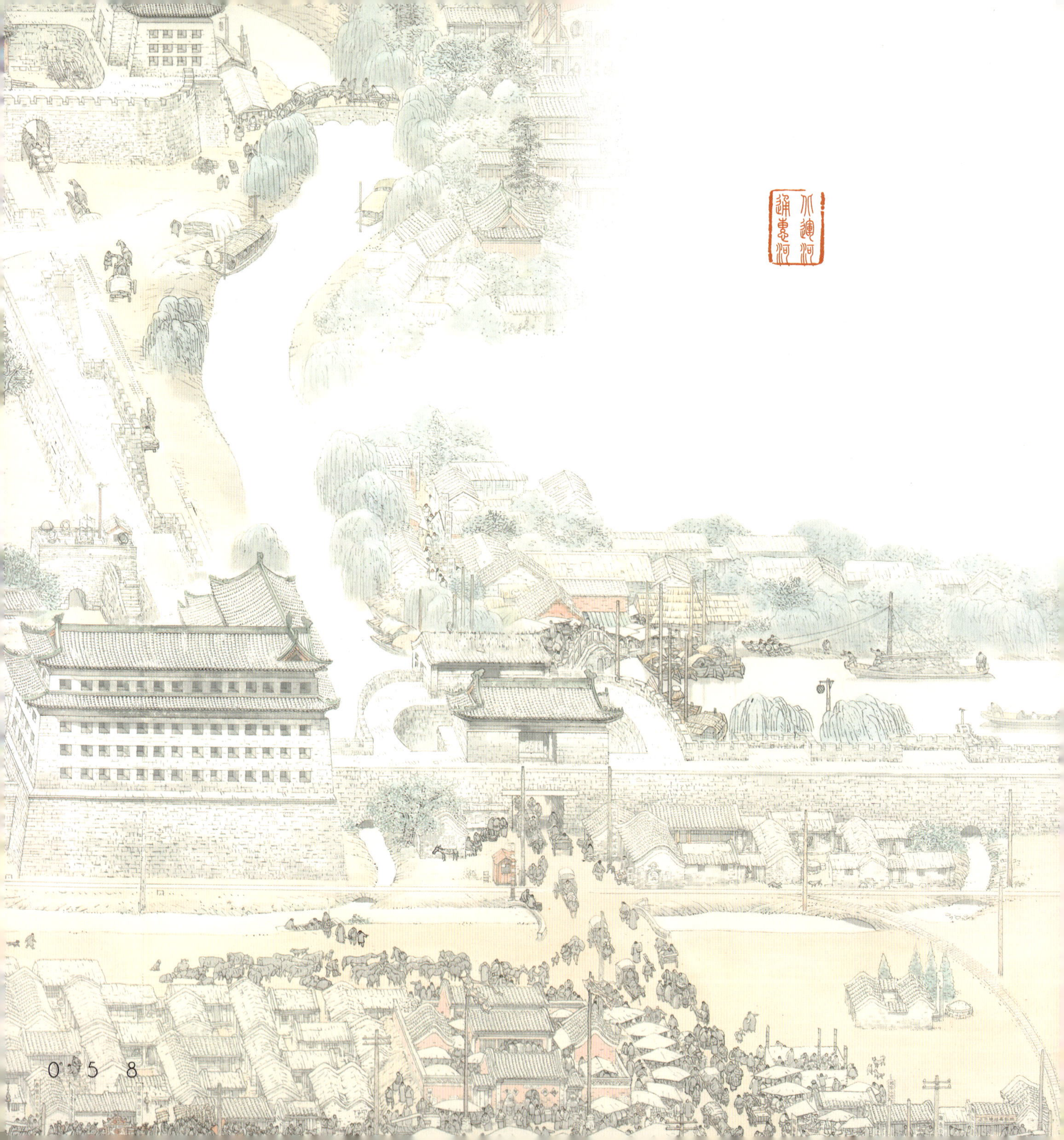
北運河
通惠河

Scan QR code for VR experience

Tonghui River of the North Canal River System

By the time when Beijing was made capital of the Yuan Dynasty, the Beijing-Hangzhou Grand Canal connected to Jiangnan (the southern region of the Yangtze River) was completed. In order to include the water system of the Capital City in the Grand Canal, the Yuan irrigationist Guo Shoujing had Tonghui River dug. By connecting Jishuitan to Tongzhou district, Tonghui River, together with the water system of the Inner City, became the main components of the North Canal, eventually facilitating the transport of freight goods from the prosperous Jiangnan region to Dadu of the Yuan Dynasty; which played quite an important role in securing the capital's food supply and was therefore considered one of the key economic lifelines of Beijing.

北运河－通惠河

元代定都北京后，连通江南与京城的京杭大运河便全线贯通了。为将北京城内水系与京杭大运河连通，元代水利专家郭守敬主持修建的漕运河道——通惠河，由此也形成了北京最主要的北运河水系。它打通了从通州到积水潭的水道，使富庶江南的物资可以直抵元大都城里，对保障首都经济发挥了极为重要的作用，是北京的一条经济命脉。

扫码观看现在的漕运码头

The Waterway of the Moats

Beijing has a sophisticatedly arranged surface drainage system. The surface currents in the Forbidden City were joined by the inner and outer Jinshui Rivers to flow along the Imperial City wall until they reached the moat south of the Capital City. The moat was joined by other different surface waters before converging into the Tonghui River east of Beijing at Tongzhou district. Beijing's water system was formed at this point, featuring moats surrounding the Imperial and Capital Cities, as well as many other rivers and lakes downtown linked by canals.

护城河水道

北京城有一套非常科学的排水系统，内外金水河在宫城和皇城内外流淌，紫禁城内的积潦最终都汇入其中，在流经大半个故宫后，南下经水道流入都城外的护城河。护城河则与众多地表水系相连，最终汇入通惠河，下接京东通州的京杭大运河，形成了护城河围绕皇城及都城、运河串联城区河湖的城市水系格局。

Yan Mountains and Taihang Mountains

  Beijing is located on the northern edge of the North China Plain, with a terrain high in the northwest and low in the southeast, bordering the Bohai Sea to the east, the North China Plain to the south, the Western Hills (part of the Taihang Mountains) to its west, and the Jundu Mountain (part of the Yan Mountains) to its north.

  The Taihang Mountains stretch hundreds of kilometers from Henan and Hebei provinces to the southwest of Beijing. They were considered natural defensive barriers west of the capital. Among the ridges lies the Great Wall. The famous Zijing pass was a vital route between Beijing and Shanxi province.

  The terrain of the Yan Mountains has been moderately gentle, but still lined with the Great Wall to guard against nomads' assaults from the north. Upon the ranges of the Yan Mountains sit Juyongguan, Xifengkou, and Gubeikou as well as other famous passes. Among them, the Shanhaiguan and Juyongguan passes were of the most military significance.

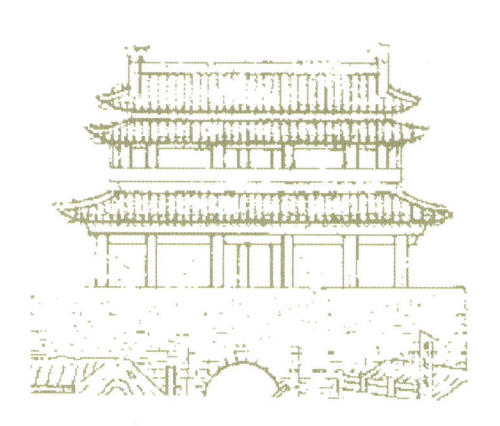

燕山－太行山脉

北京地处华北平原的北部边缘，地势西北高、东南低，东部为渤海，南部为华北平原，西部是西山，属于太行山山脉，北部是军都山，属于燕山山脉。

太行山山脉从河南经河北到北京西南，绵延数百公里，多崇山峻岭，是护卫京都的天然屏障，有长城修筑其间，最著名的关隘为紫荆关，是北京通往山西的要道。

燕山山脉相对平缓，长城沿山脊蜿蜒分布，用于防止北方游牧民族入侵。燕山山脉上有居庸关、喜峰口、古北口等著名关隘。其中，山海关和居庸关是最重要的军事关隘。

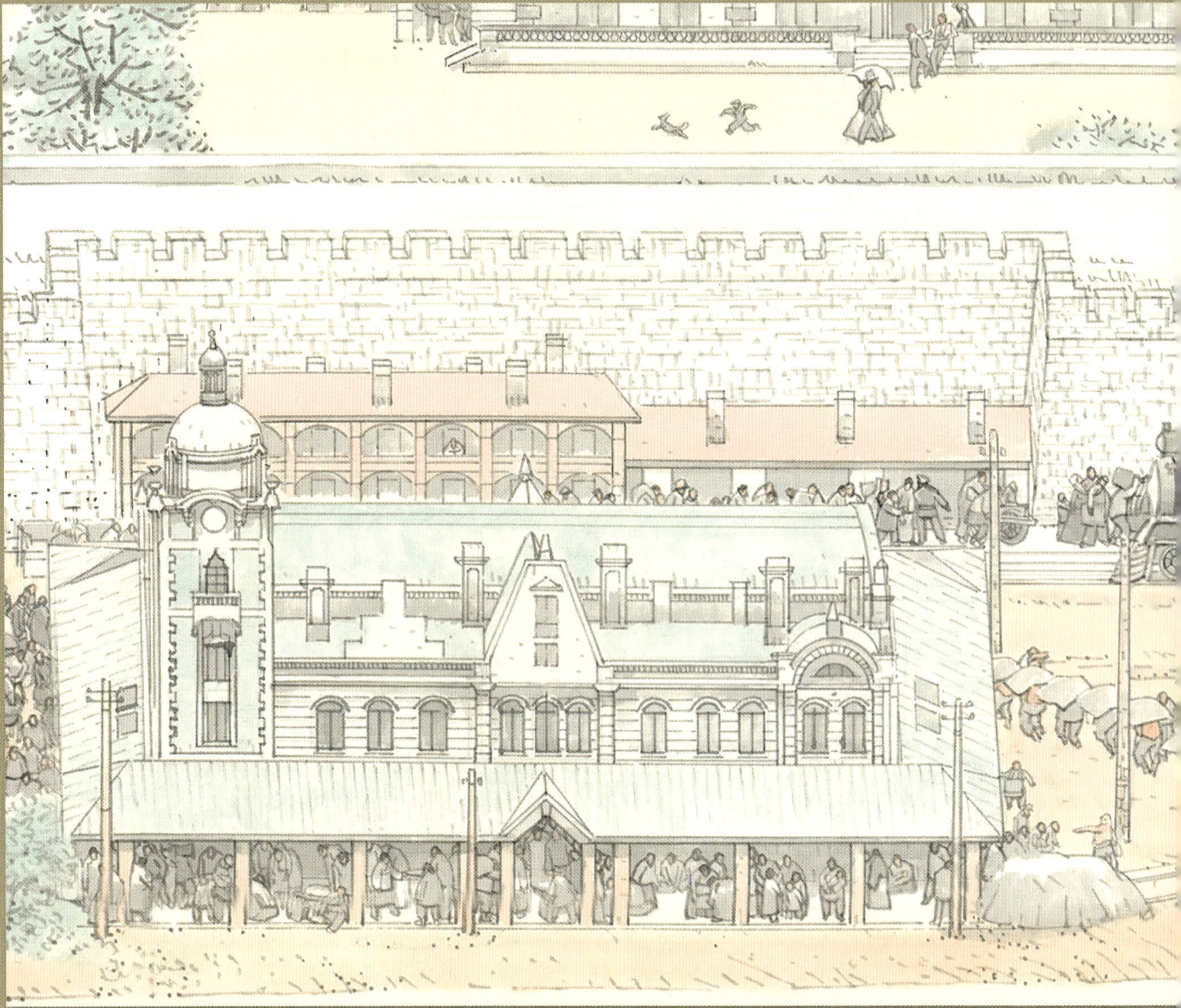

第二章 近代化进程

CHAPTER 2 THE MODERNIZATION PROCESS

Between 1910 and 1920, political forces of different stances came on stage in Beijing.

The waning Qing Dynasty struggled to maintain its final dignity. Imperial palaces and gardens all over the Capital City apparently reminded people of their former glory. The institutions of modernization set up in the late Qing reforms kept struggling to maintain a mode of governance which had been lasting for 2,000 years.

As democracy and republicanism were introduced, modern institutions such as the Presidential Palace, the Congress and the Army Administration were established. Politicians and members of Congress were seen in Beijing with their ideas and strategies for governing the country. Once again, the city became the stage for various political forces to act on.

After the Boxer Uprising in 1900, the Legation Quarter became an "enclave" de facto as newly planned blocks, Western-style architectures, and advanced municipal facilities were brought in as well as modern financial, police, and administrative systems established in the ancient city of Beijing.

Following the 1911 Revolution, the authority of the Republic of China carried on Beijing's urbanization transformation. More and more neighborhoods have been equipped with municipal facilities such as roads, streetlights, and sewerage. The application of new means of transportation and communication has changed the lifestyles of ordinary people. With the emergence of parks, public libraries, and museums, the urbanization process of Beijing had been gathering momentum.

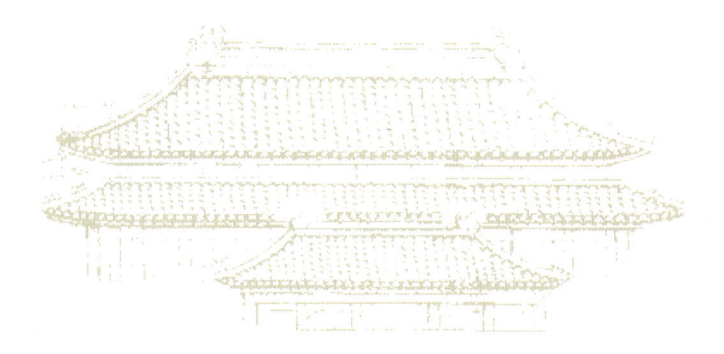

以北京城为基点，以1910—1920年的十年时间为横切面，我们可以看到这个时期涌动着几股力量，都在这座城市中以自己的方式表现着各不相同的政治姿态。

日薄西山的清王朝艰难维持着自己最后的尊严——坐落在京城各处的宫阙、园囿似乎还在提醒着人们它们往日的辉煌；清末新政中设立的近代化机构还在借助文化惯性维护着一套存续两千年的管理体系。

民主、共和的新风吹来，总统府、国会、陆军部等具有近代性质的政府机构顺势出现，政要、议员带着自己的治国方略出现在北京，北京再次成为各种政治势力角逐的舞台。

庚子事变后，东交民巷的使馆区成了北京城里的"国中之国"，新式街区、西洋建筑、先进的市政设施、近代的金融与警政系统，在这座古老城市落地。

辛亥革命后，民国政府接过了北京近代化进程的接力棒，继续开展城市化改造。马路、街灯、排水系统等市政设施被推广应用到更多街区，新式交通工具、通信工具的应用改变了普通市民的生活方式。而公园、公共图书馆、博物馆的出现，使北京迎来了城市近代化加速发展的新阶段。

盛景犹存的古都景观
MAGNIFICENT IMPERIAL LANDSCAPES

The Temple of Heaven

The Temple of Heaven was where emperors of the Ming and Qing dynasties prayed to the heavenly god for a good harvest. It has been the largest and most intact altar complex in China so far. The two main structures, the Circular Mound Altar and the Altar of Praying for Grain are respectively used for offering sacrifices to heaven during the winter solstice and praying for grains during early spring. The landmark Hall of Prayer for Good Harvests is located on the latter. In traditional Chinese culture, an emperor's worship of heaven was considered the most solemn ritual. More importantly, his throne and power were highly endorsed by that ceremony. On January 1,1918, it was officially announced a public park by the Ministry of Internal Affairs of the Republic of China. The Temple of Heaven was inscribed on the World Heritage List in 1998.

Scan QR code for VR experience

天坛

天坛是明清帝王祭天祈谷的场所，是中国现存规模最大、形制最完备的祭坛建筑群。圜丘坛和祈谷坛是天坛里面最主要的建筑，分别用于"冬至祭天"和"孟春祈谷"，标志性建筑"祈年殿"就在祈谷坛上。在中国传统文化中，帝王祭天是最为隆重庄严的祭祀典礼，皇帝通过祭天仪式来宣示自己的身份与权力。1918年1月1日，在国民政府内务部的主持下，天坛被辟为公园正式对外开放。1998年，天坛已被联合国教科文组织列入《世界遗产名录》。

扫码观看现在的天坛

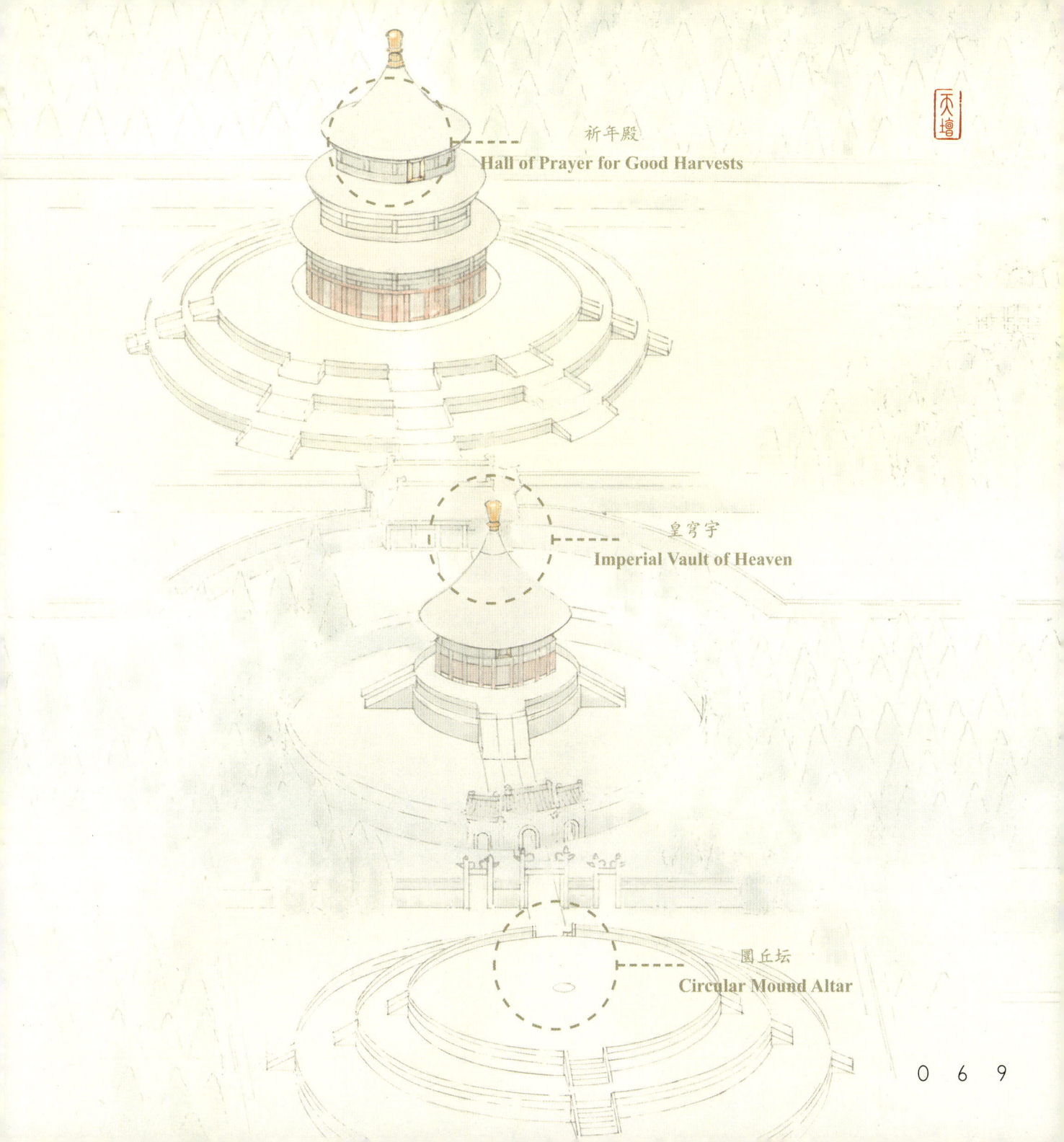

祈年殿
Hall of Prayer for Good Harvests

皇穹宇
Imperial Vault of Heaven

圜丘坛
Circular Mound Altar

日坛
Ritan(Temple of the Sun)

☉ Nine Altars

In Beijing, there were said to be nine altars and eight temples. In addition to the Temple of Heaven, there are also temples for the earth, the sun, the moon, and agriculture. They were particularly built for the Ming and Qing emperors to worship those gods respectively.

Scan QR code for VR experience

扫码观看现在的日坛公园

⊙ 北京"九坛"

在北京城有"九坛八庙"之说,除了天坛,还有地坛、日坛、月坛、先农坛等,是明清两朝帝王们祭天、地、日、月、山川、太岁等神祇而特意建造的。

The Imperial Ancestral Temple

Since the Zhou Dynasty, emperors of successive dynasties worshipped their ancestors at the Imperial Ancestral Temple. Built in the Ming and Qing Dynasties, the Imperial Ancestral Temple in Beijing is the largest and most intact imperial temple for ancestral worship in China. Except for the emperors and empresses, imperial clansmen and meritorious officials during that period may find their place there, too. In 1924, the site was turned into a park named Heping (meaing peace in Chinese), and in 1950, it was transformed into the Beijing Working People's Cultural Palace.

Scan QR code for VR experience

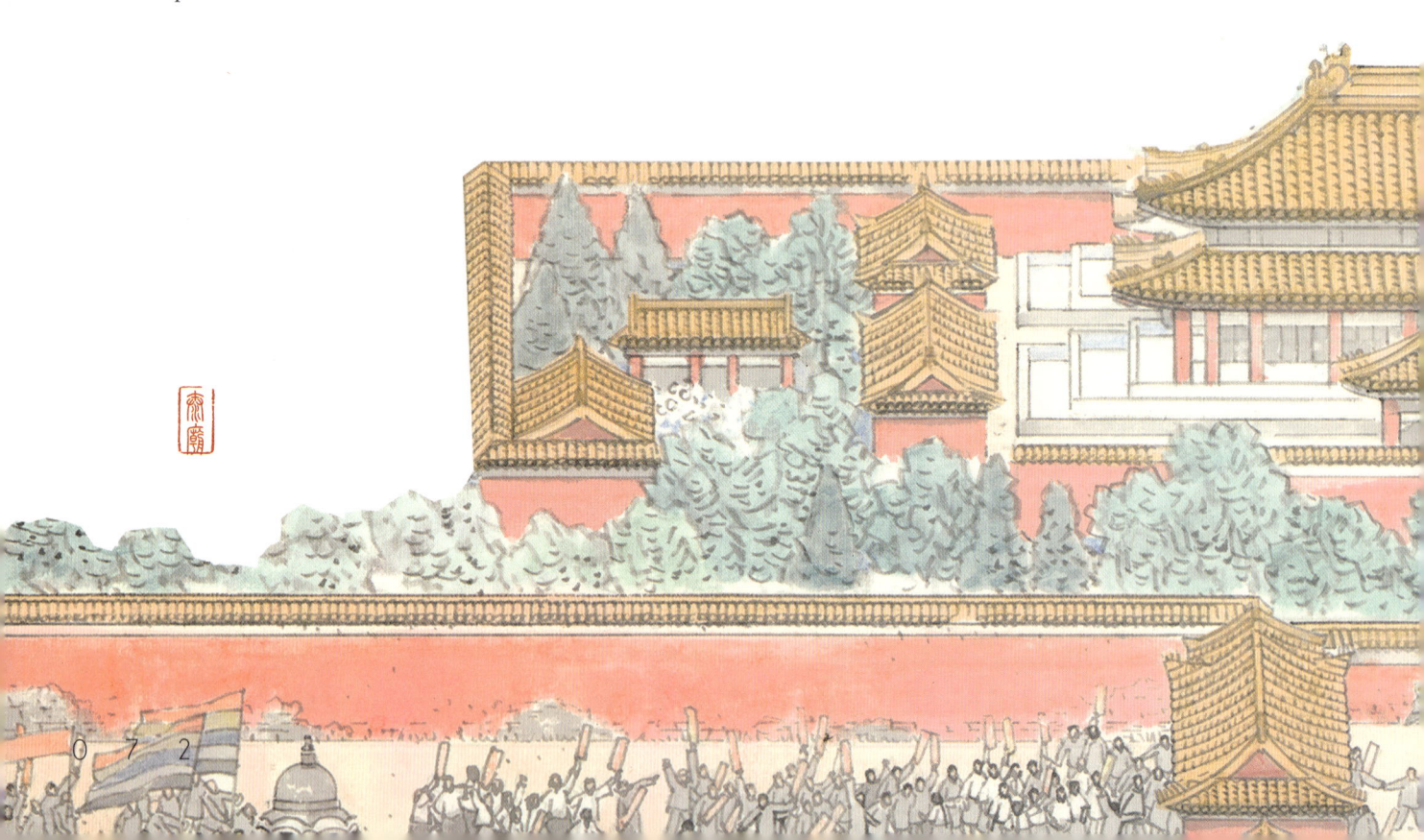

太庙

　　太庙自周代以来即皇家宗庙，是历代帝王代表国家祭祀祖先的场所。北京的太庙是明清时期建造、现存规模最大、格局最完整的皇家祭祀祖先的庙宇。明清时期的太庙除供奉历代帝王，还祭祀宗室、功臣。1924年，太庙被辟为和平公园，1950年改为北京市劳动人民文化宫。

扫码观看现在的太庙

Scan QR code for VR experience

The Altar of Land and Grain

The Altar of Land and Grain was the place for worshipping gods in ancient China. In traditional Chinese culture, it was considered a solemn ritual offering sacrifices to the Gods of Soil (*She*) and of Grain (*Ji*), for they were believed to be capable of bringing good weather and peace to the country and its people. Worshipping of the two gods were carried out on two different altars until the Ming rulers combined them into one. The site was repurposed as the Central Park (now Zhongshan Park in Beijing) on October 10, 1914. In addition to a built-in mini public library, it was the place where many cultural salons and historically significant gatherings were held.

⊙ **Earth of Five Colors**

According to the theory of *Yin-yang* and five elements, there are earth of five colors on the altar of Land and Grain, including blue, red, white, black, and yellow.

扫码观看现在的社稷坛

社稷坛

社稷坛是中国古代祭祀社神和稷神的场所。在中国传统文化中,"社"为土地之祖,"稷"为五谷之神,祭祀社稷被视为帝王重要的礼制活动,以求风调雨顺、国泰民安。以前的社稷坛分为社坛和稷坛两座坛,明朝在北京建造社稷坛时将社神和稷神合在一座坛加以祭祀。1914年10月10日,社稷坛被辟为中央公园(今中山公园),许多文化沙龙和重要集会都在这里举行。公园内还设立了"中央公园图书阅览所"向市民开放。

⊙ 社稷坛上的五色土

社稷坛的坛面上按照中国传统的阴阳五行学说铺设了青、红、白、黑、黄五色土壤。

五色土
Earth of Five Colors

The Temple of Past Monarchs

The Temple of Pass Monarchs was where the Chinese ancestors Yellow and Flame emperors as well as ancient Chinese emperors were honored during the Ming and Qing Dynasties. It was the only imperial temple dedicated to worshipping the emperors of the past dynasties in China. Its existence was proof of the continuity of Chinese history and culture, which could be traced to the same origin. The temple enshrined worship tablets of 188 emperors and 79 eminent generals and ministers, ranging from the Three Sovereigns and Five Emperors, to emperor Chongzhen of the Ming Dynasty. After the Qing emperor's abdication in 1912, the place had gradually become obsolete. Later, it was used as the schoolhouse by various bodies in succession. In 2000, the temple went through some renovations before reopening to the public.

历代帝王庙

历代帝王庙是明清时期祭祀中华炎黄祖先和历代帝王的皇家庙宇，也是国内现存唯一一座专门祭祀历代帝王的庙宇，是中华历史文化一脉相承、连绵不断的证明。历代帝王庙供奉着从三皇五帝到明朝崇祯的中国历史上一百八十八位皇帝和七十九位历代功臣名将。1912年，清帝退位后，历代帝王庙逐渐荒废，先后成为不同学校的校舍。2000年，历代帝王庙经修缮后对外开放。

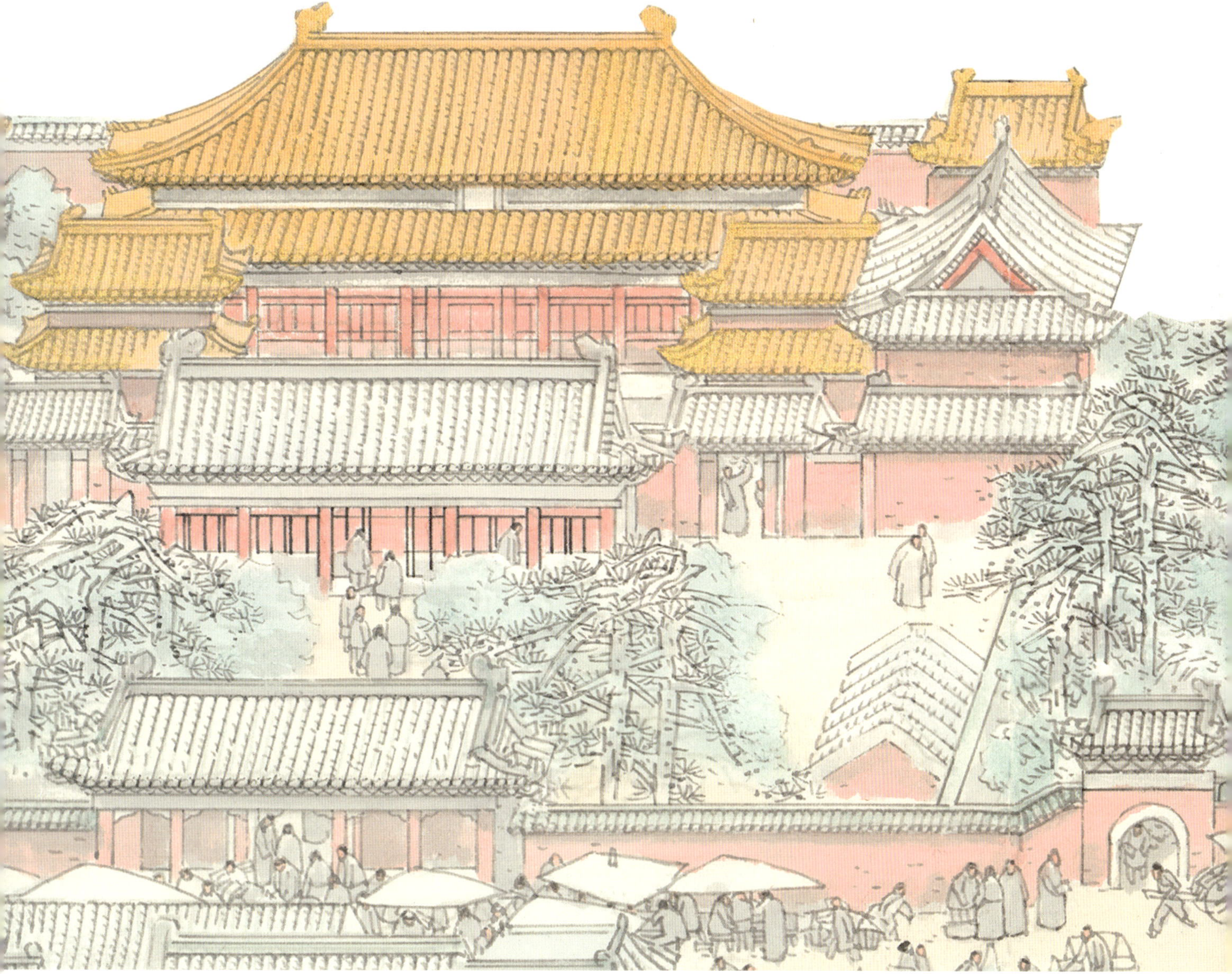

觀象臺

The Beijing Ancient Observatory

The Beijing Ancient Observatory is located next to the southeast corner tower of the Inner City. As the royal observatory of the Ming and Qing dynasties, it is one of the oldest existing observatories in the world. In traditional Chinese culture, observing celestial objects for calendaring and time service was regarded as supreme imperial power.

During the Qing emperor Kangxi's reign, Johann Adam Schall von Bell (Chinese name Tang Ruowang), a foreign missionary, introduced Western astronomy into Chinese calendaring. Later, several large-sized copper astronomical instruments of both Chinese and Western designs were manufactured and set up at the observatory.

When the Eight-Power Allied Forces invaded Beijing in 1900, those instruments were carved up by the German and French troops. Under the terms of the *Treaty of Versailles*, some of the stolen pieces were returned to China after World War I and reinstalled at their original site.

观象台

观象台位于北京内城东南角楼旁，是明清时期的皇家天文台，也是世界上现存最古老的天文台之一。在中国传统文化中，观天象以制历授时是帝王至高无上的权力。清康熙帝在位期间，接受了西洋传教士汤若望的建议，改用欧洲天文学方法计算时历，并先后设计制作了多组大型铜制的中西方天文仪器放置于观象台。

1900年，八国联军入侵北京时，这些天文仪器被德、法两国瓜分。第一次世界大战后，根据《凡尔赛和约》规定，被抢走的一部分天文仪器被陆续归还我国，并被重新安放在观象台上。

The Old Summer Palace

Yuanmingyuan (the Garden of Perfect Brightness, a.k.a. Old Summer Palace), a monumental imperial garden built in the Qing Dynasty, is composed of three gardens adjacent to one another, namely, Yuanmingyuan, Changchunyuan, and Qichunyuan. It perfectly inherited the Chinese gardening tradition while drew inspiration from Western architectural styles. Being a comprehensive expression of the best techniques in garden making at that time, it was lauded as the "garden of myriad gardens".

During the Second Opium War, the Old Summer Palace was ravaged, all her treasures looted, and all buildings within burnt down. Even though the palace was acknowledged by the authority of the Republic of China as the imperial property of the Qing court, the fact that its woods, stones, ancient trees, and tablets had been encroaching away all along was the reason why only the ruins of the European Palaces remained standing.

The site was listed as a major historical and cultural site protected at the national level. It was opened to the public in June, 1988, and selected as one of the Sixteen New Sights of Beijing in 2010.

圆明园

圆明园，是清代建造的大型皇家园林，由圆明园、长春园和绮春园组成，合称"圆明三园"。园内既有中国传统园林景色，又有西方园林建筑精品，集中了当时世界造园艺术的巅峰之作，被誉为"万园之园"。

第二次鸦片战争时期，英法联军侵入北京，圆明园惨遭劫难，园内珍宝被抢掠一空，而园中建筑又被焚毁。民国时期，虽然圆明园仍属皇室私产，但园内木料砖石、古树碑碣被官民抢运殆尽，最终只留下西洋楼遗址矗立在那里。

现在的圆明园遗址已经被国家保护起来，成为圆明园遗址公园，并被列为全国重点文物保护单位，于1988年6月对外开放，2010年又被评为"北京新十六景"之一，成为北京园林中的一颗耀眼明珠。

The Summer Palace

Formerly known as Qingyiyuan (the Garden of Clear Ripples), the Summer Palace was among the five imperial gardens for short stays during the Qing Dynasty. Built on the basis of Kunming Lake and Wanshoushan (Longevity Hill), it is now the most well-preserved royal palace and lauded as a museum of imperial gardens.

Towards the late Qing Dynasty, emperor Guangxu spent huge on renovating the Summer Palace for the birthday celebration of the Empress Dowager Cixi. After the Qing Dynasty, the Summer Palace was managed by the Imperial Household Department for it was still a private property of Puyi, the former emperor. In 1913, in order to subsidize the garden's finances, the Qing royal family turned it into a tourist attraction that charged admission fees. In 1928, the Summer Palace was confiscated by the National Government of Nanjing and officially became a public park.

It kept functioning as a park after 1949, and was listed as a major historical and cultural site protected at the national level in 1961. Before being included in the list of 5A-level scenic areas in 2007, it was inscribed on the World Heritage List in 1998.

⊙ Three Hills and Five Gardens

Between emperor Kangxi and Qianlong's reigns, there were altogether three hills and five gardens built in the western suburbs, namely, the Longevity Hill, Xiangshan (the Fragrant Hill), the Jade Spring Hill, the Summer Palace, Jingyiyuan (the Garden of Tranquility and Pleasure), Jingmingyuan (the Garden of Tranquility and Brightness), Changchunyuan (the Garden of Everlasting Spring), and the Garden of Perfect Brightness, when Qingyiyuan was completed in 1750. They formed a unique layout of royal summer resorts and recreational gardens covering an area of nearly 20 kilometers in length.

颐和园

颐和园，是清朝皇家园林中"三山五园"的代表作，原称清漪园，清后期改称颐和园。它是以昆明湖、万寿山为基址建成的一座大型山水园林，也是目前保存最完整的一座皇家行宫御苑，有"皇家园林博物馆"之誉。

清朝末年，光绪帝为了给慈禧太后祝寿，曾用重金修整颐和园。清朝灭亡后，颐和园作为皇帝私产，仍由清室内务府管理。1913年，为补贴园林财政，清室将颐和园改为售票参观。1928年，颐和园被南京国民政府接收，正式成为公园。

新中国成立后，这里仍然作为公园。1961年，颐和园被列为第一批全国重点文物保护单位；1998年，又被联合国教科文组织列入《世界遗产名录》；2007年，再被列为国家5A级旅游景区。

⊙三山五园

清代，自康熙至乾隆，在北京西郊修建了多处皇家园林，乾隆十五年（1750）颐和园前身清漪园建成后，西郊以万寿山、香山、玉泉山，颐和园、静宜园、静明园、畅春园和圆明园"三山五园"的皇家园林格局正式形成，这片长达二十公里的皇家园林区，成为皇家避暑、游憩之地。

应时演变的近代机构
EVOLVING MODERN INSTITUTIONS

The Ministry of Foreign Affairs

The Ministry of Foreign Affairs of the Qing authority was located in a Chinese-style building at Dongtangzi *hutong*, with a plaque on the main gate inscribed with four Chinese characters "*zhong wai ti fu*", standing for good wishes for global peace and happiness. The increasingly frequent contacts with the West had brought fatal impacts on the tributary-based institution of the Qing Dynasty. Following the Second Opium War, the Qing authority established the General Management Office of Affairs Concerning All Nations (*zongli yamen*), which was China's first official diplomatic agency of modern times. According to the *Protocol of 1901*, *zongli yamen* was restructured as the Ministry of Foreign Affairs to run diplomatic affairs on behalf of the state and the government, keeping in line with international practices.

外务部

东堂子胡同中,有一座正门挂着"中外禔福"匾额的中式建筑,这便是清政府的外交机构。近代以来,与西方的频繁交往给清王朝纳贡体制带来了致命冲击。第二次鸦片战争后,清政府成立了中国第一个正式的近代外交机构——总理各国事务衙门,专门处理外交事务。1901年,根据《辛丑条约》,清政府将总理各国事务衙门改为外务部,作为中国的正式外交机构开始处理与海外各国交往事宜,表明中国外交已经走上了更加规范的轨道。

The Model Prison

The Model Prison of the Capital located south of Xuanwumen Gate was a new prison prototype set up by the Qing authority. Towards the late Qing Dynasty, the Ministry of Punishment was transformed into the Ministry of Law, and model prisons were ordered to be set up in all Chinese provinces. The construction of the Model Prison of the Capital began in 1910, and in late 1912 it was taken over and put into use by the Ministry of Justice of the Republic of China who renamed it the Beijing Prison. It was equipped with an admonishment room, a prison factory, a library, a reading room, and visiting rooms, as well as separate cells for male, female, sick, and juvenile inmates, just like prisons today.

模范监狱

京师模范监狱坐落于宣武门外菜市口以南，是清政府修建的一所新式监狱。清朝末年，政府推行新政，改刑部为法部，并通令各省一律筹办新式监狱。京师模范监狱于1910年动工，1912年末由中华民国司法部接管并投入使用，更名北京监狱。模范监狱内设有教诲所、囚犯工场、书籍室、阅览室、囚人接见室等场所，还分设男监、女监，并单设病监、幼年监等，已经具备现代监狱的各项功能。

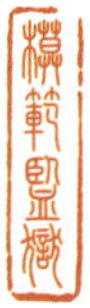

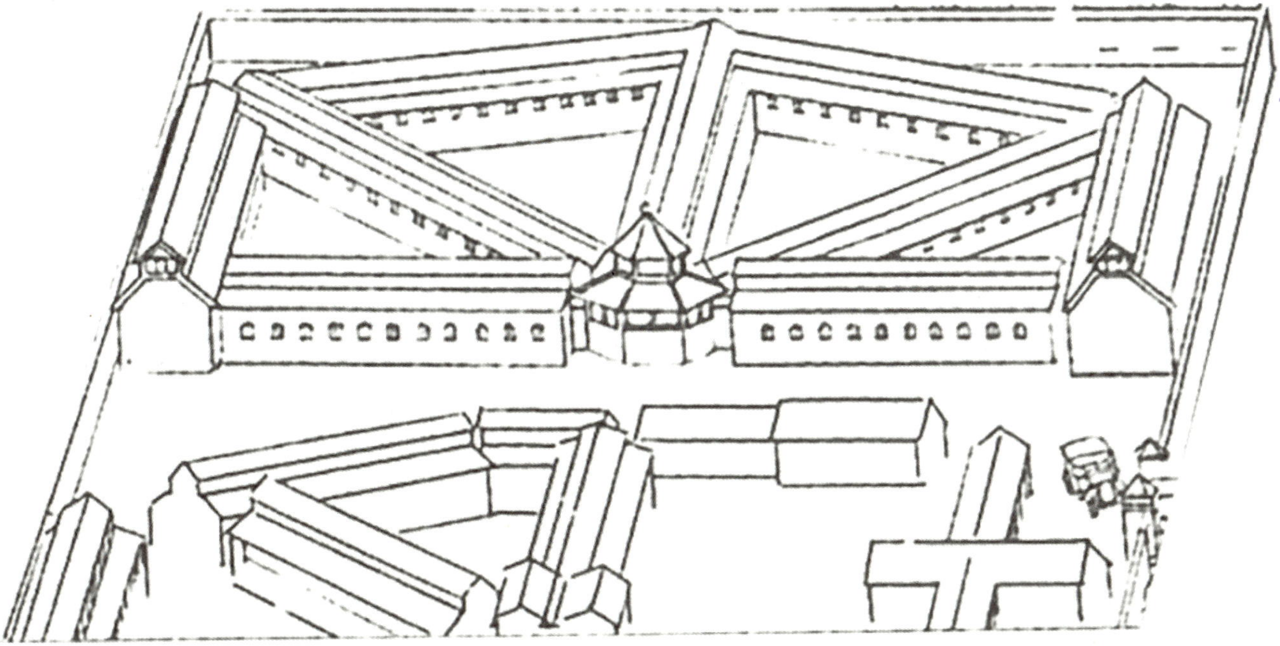

⊙ The Army Administration

In 1906, a recently brought up baroque building on the site of the residence of Prince He at Tieshizi *hutong* became the office of the Army Administration and the army academy for the nobles. Yuan Shikai turned the place into his Presidential Palace and the State Council in 1912 but moved out the next year. In 1924, Duan Qirui served as the acting Chief Executive of the Republic of China there. When Renmin University of China was founded in 1950, the site became its earliest campus.

⊙ 陆军部大楼

1906年,清政府在铁狮子胡同原和亲王府修建了一片巴洛克式建筑作为陆军部大楼和陆军贵胄学堂。1912年,袁世凯在此设立总统府和国务院,1913年迁出。1924年段祺瑞曾在此设立执政府。1950年,中国人民大学在此成立。

The Central Military Training Department

The Central Military Training Department was the administrative institution for military training in the late Qing Dynasty, which played an important role in modernizing the Chinese army. Since the results of military training on the provincial level called upon by the late Qing reforms in 1901 fell short of expectations, the Central Military Training Department was set up to promote the training of raw recruits throughout the country. From its establishment in 1903 to incorporation into the Army Administration in 1906, the Central Military Training Department unified the formations nationwide with reference to Western standards, formulated the system of officers and ranks, set standards for the army academy, and detailed rules for sending military officers to study abroad. By the time of its departmental consolidation with the Army Administration in 1906, the main body of the new army was already well-trained and eventually became the force to overthrow the Qing authority.

练兵处

练兵处是清末新军编练的领导机关，在促进中国陆军近代化方面起了举足轻重的作用。1901 年，清末新政下令全国编练新军，但各省编练情况并不理想。1903 年，清政府设置练兵处，以推进全国新兵编练。从 1903 年设立到 1906 年合并到陆军部，练兵处在三年时间里参照西方标准统一了全国新军编制，制定了新军军官和军衔制度，统一了陆军学堂的学制，拟定了派遣陆军留学办法。截至 1906 年练兵处合并到陆军部前，清末新军主体已经基本练成，最终，这些新军成为推翻清朝统治的一支重要力量。

怀仁堂
Huairentang

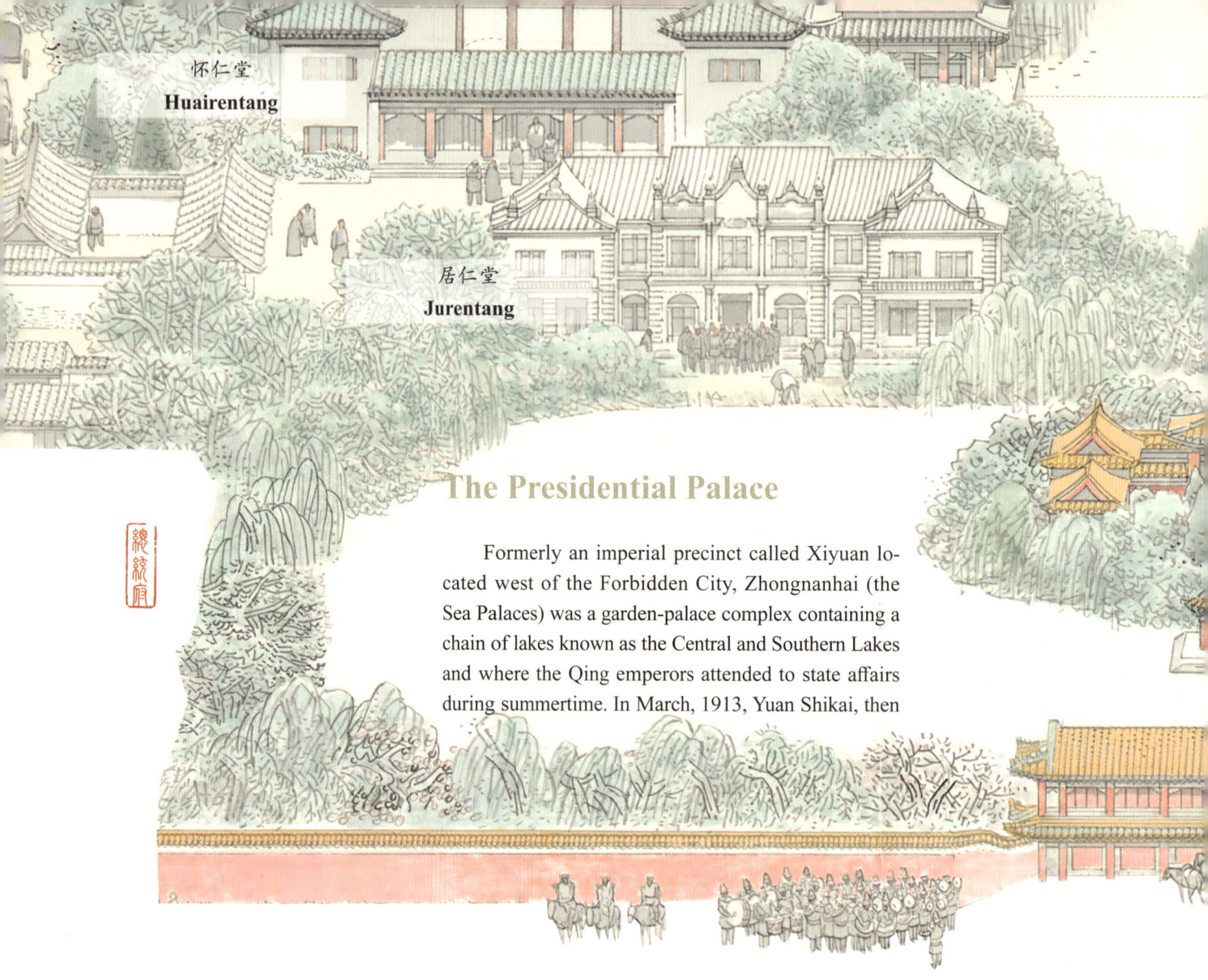

居仁堂
Jurentang

The Presidential Palace

Formerly an imperial precinct called Xiyuan located west of the Forbidden City, Zhongnanhai (the Sea Palaces) was a garden-palace complex containing a chain of lakes known as the Central and Southern Lakes and where the Qing emperors attended to state affairs during summertime. In March, 1913, Yuan Shikai, then Provisional President of the Republic of China, made Zhongnanhai his new Presidential Palace. After moving in, he took up Huairentang (the Palace Steeped in Compassion), which had been Cixi's sleeping chamber before, as his new office. The building that looks identical to Haiyantang (the European Palaces) at the Old Summer Palace was refurbished as the reception hall and renamed Jurentang (the Hall Where Benevolence Resides). Yuan also had the former building of Baoyuelou restructured into Xinhuamen Gate, which became the formal entrance to the Sea Palaces. From this time on till the founding of the Nanjing-based Nationalist Government in 1928, the place functioned as the center of power of the Republic of China.

紫光阁
Ziguangge
(Throne Hall of the Effalgent Pole-star)

瀛台
Yingtai
(Sea Terrace Island)

新华门
Xinhua Gate

总统府

中南海位于皇家园囿西苑（今前三海），由中海和南海构成，是清朝皇帝避暑、听政的场所。1913年3月，时任中华民国临时大总统的袁世凯将总统府迁入中南海，将慈禧寝宫仪鸾殿改名为"怀仁堂"并在此办公，又将仿照圆明园西洋楼的海晏堂更名"居仁堂"作为会客场所，还将宝月楼改建为总统府正门命名为"新华门"。从这时起到1928年国民政府南迁，这里一直是中华民国的权力中心。

國會議場

The Congress Hall

In April 1912, the Provisional Government of the Republic of China in Beijing schemed up for Congress. The Advisory Council of the late Qing was chosen for the House of Senates and the original site of the Finance School and the Law School of the Capital were for the House of Representatives, plus the Congress Hall. Completed in 1913, the Congress Hall was a typical Western-style architecture and probably the earliest assembly building in the Republic of China period. In 1924, Congress was dissolved. The site of the Congress Hall was transformed into the Law School of Beiping University in 1928, and in 1946, the Fourth School of Peking University. After 1949, it became the headquarters of the Xinhua News Agency, in the courtyard of which the site of the Congress Hall could still be found.

国会议场

1912年4月，中华民国北京临时政府开始筹建国会，选定清末咨议机关资政院旧址作为参议院院址，东侧的清末京师财政学堂和法律学堂则作为众议院的基址并增设国会议场。1913年，国会议场建成，是民国时期较早的会堂式建筑，也是当时北京西洋建筑的代表作。1924年国会解散。1928年，此地改为北平大学法学院，1946年改称北京大学第四院。新中国成立后，这里改为新华通讯社，现在的国会议场旧址就在新华通讯社院内。

朱启钤在正阳门改造工程现场
Zhu Qiqian supervising the reconstruction project of Zhengyangmen Gate

The Beijing Municipal Office

The Beijing Municipal Office was established in August, 1914, responsible for the city's urban planning and infrastructure construction. Zhu Qiqian, then Chief Director of the Department of Internal Affairs, acted as its first supervisor. Aiming at modernizing Beijing, Zhu oversaw projects such as remodeling Zhengyangmen Gate; building five main streets surrounding the Imperial City block from previous dead ends, including Nanchangjie, Beichangjie, Nanchizi, Beichizi, and Jingshanqianjie; the refunctioning of the Temple of Land and Grain into Central Park and the Temple of Agriculture into Chengnan Park; and the construction of a trendy commercial block, i.e., building Xiangchang New District into a poilot urban area. With dozens of urban planning projects carry out, the Beijing Municipal Office helped transform this ancient capital into a modern city.

京都市政公所

1914年8月，在内务总长朱启钤的推动下，京都市政公所成立，负责北京城市规划与基础设施建设，朱启钤兼任督办，开始对北京进行现代化改革。首先，朱启钤推动了正阳门改造工程，打通了南北长街、南北池子、景山前街，开辟改造社稷坛为中央公园，先农坛为城南公园；其次，启动了"模范市区"建设项目，将外城香厂地区打造成了新的商业街区。京都市政公所的一系列市政规划项目，加快了北京由"古都"向"近代城市"转型的进程。

京兆尹公署

京兆尹公署是民国初年北京地方最高行政机关，它的前身为明清时期的顺天府。顺天府下辖的大兴、宛平两县与中央政府一同对北京城行使管理权。1914年10月，顺天府改为京兆，设立京兆尹公署为其行政机关，但管理上仍沿用旧制，由地方公署与中央政府一起管理。到1921年，北洋政府将北京定为京都特别市。1928年，南京国民政府改北京为"北平市"，北京才有了首任市长。

The Mayor's Office of the Capital City of Beijing

During the first few years of the Republic of China, Shuntianfu, the local administrative institution of Beijing Prefecture during the Ming and Qing Dynasties, remained functional until it was substituted by Jingzhao (one of the ancient Chinese terms for the capital of a country, specifically refers to Beijing during the stated period) in October, 1914. Before that, Daxing and Wanping, the two counties under the jurisdiction of Shuntianfu, were co-managed by the central government. Now that the government office of Jingzhaoyin (i.e., the Mayor's Office of the Capital City) was set up, it still followed the old practice in which Beijing was under co-supervision by the local and central governments. The Beiyang authority established Beijing as a special administrative city in 1921. It was not until 1928 that Beijing became a city in modern sense as the Nanjing-based Nationalist Government appointed the first mayor of the city of Beiping.

097

EXOTIC EMBASSY AREA
极具风格的外国使馆 (三)

The Legation Quarter (Dongjiaominxiang *hutong*)

After the Second Opium War, foreign envoys began to have permanent residence in Beijing. As a result, legations of various countries were set up around Dongjiaominxiang hutong, Beijing's Legation Quarter close to the southern section of the Imperial City wall. "Legation Quarter occupied by the Powers shall be considered as a special area reserved for their use under exclusive control and may be defensible. Each Power shall maintain a guard in the said Quarter for the defense of its Legation." The Legation Quarter therefore became an "enclave" de facto. From then on, Western-style buildings were seen there one after another; modern municipal facilities such as roads, streetlights, tap water, and drainage systems were put into use in this part of the city. It became the early model of Beijing's modernization process.

东交民巷

第二次鸦片战争后，由于外国公使开始常驻北京，各国在紧邻皇城南城墙的东交民巷一带建立使馆。1901年，根据《辛丑条约》，西方各国将原来分散的使馆连成一片，建立起东交民巷使馆区，各国派兵驻守、自设警察、自行管理，俨然成了"国中之国"。此后，各种风格的西洋建筑相继建成，马路、街灯、自来水、排水系统等现代市政设施也投入使用，使这里率先成为城市近代化的典范。

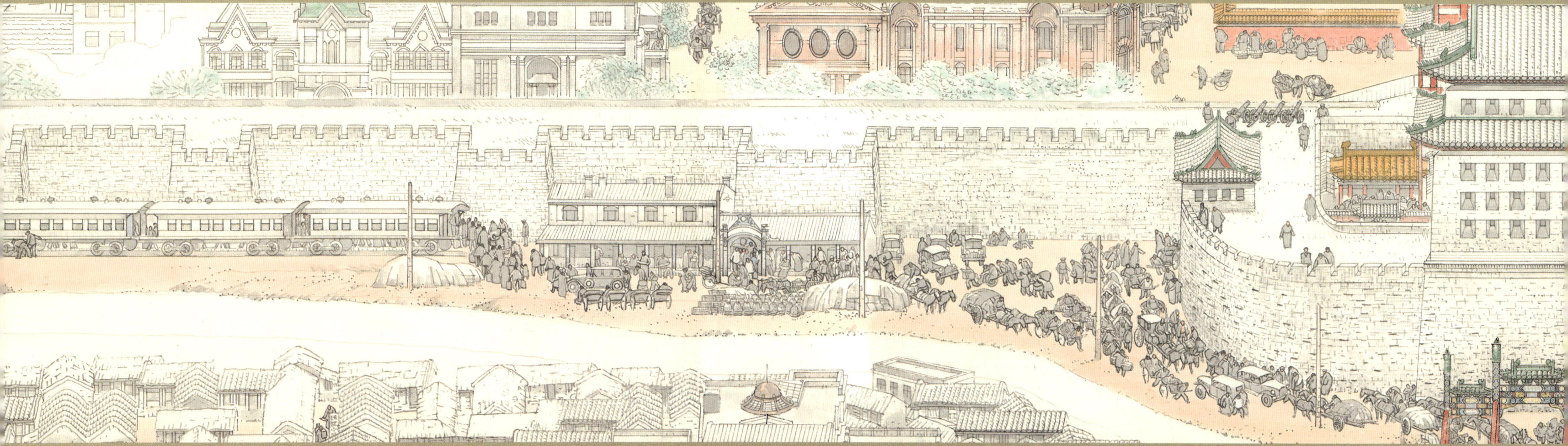

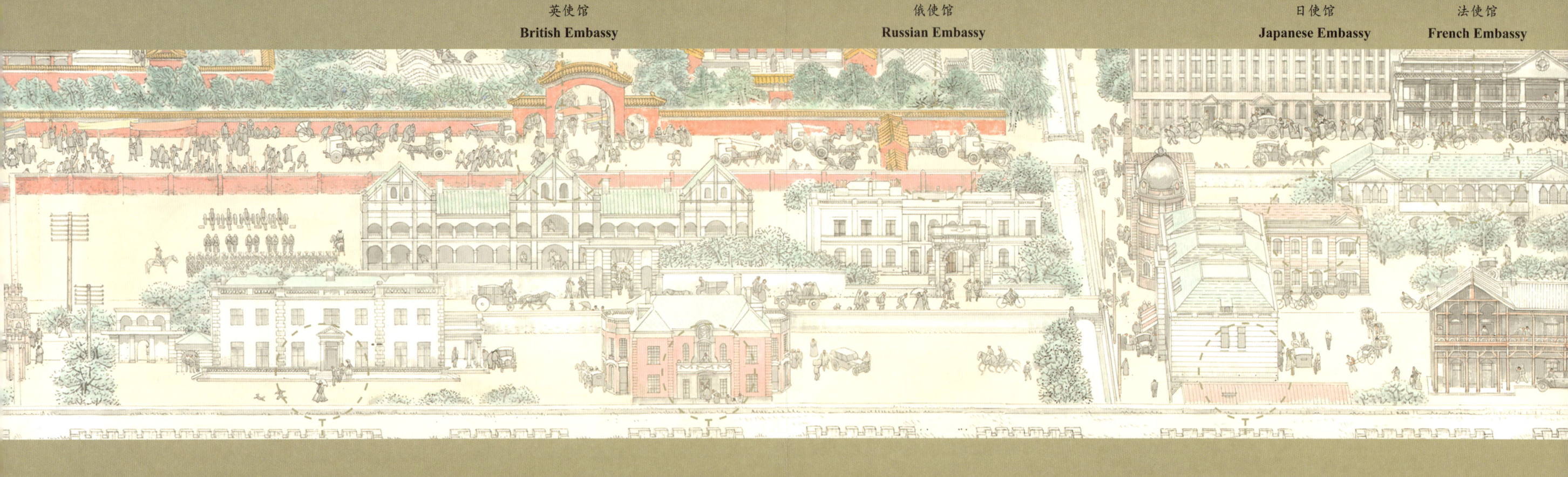

英使馆	俄使馆	日使馆	法使馆
British Embassy	Russian Embassy	Japanese Embassy	French Embassy

美使馆	荷使馆	六国饭店
American Embassy	Dutch Embassy	Grand Hotel des Wagons-Lits

⊙ **The Grand Hotel des Wagons-Lits**

Located in the Legation Quarter, the Grand Hotel des Wagons-Lits was built in 1905 as a joint venture by the United Kingdom, France, the United States, Germany, Japan, and Russia. Housing over 200 guestrooms and equipped with modern facilities such as telephones, elevators, heating, running water, and flushing toilets, the three-story brick structure was one of the tallest Western-style buildings in Beijing back then. As the pioneer of the city's Western dining and leisure trends and one of the hotspots for social activities in Beijing, the Grand Hotel des Wagons-Lits was patronized by various political figures.

意使馆
Italian Embassy

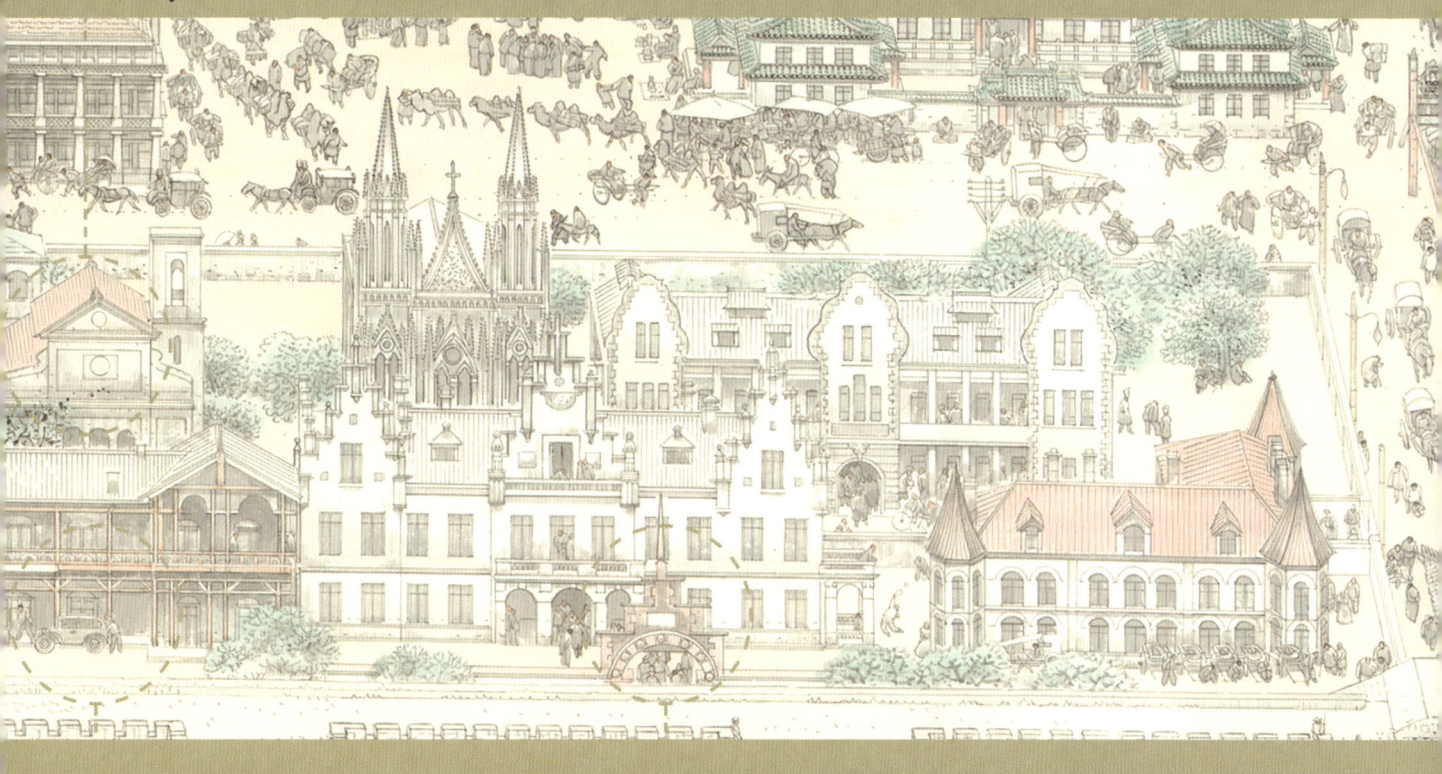

德使馆
German Embassy

比使馆
Belgian Embassy

⊙ 六国饭店

　　六国饭店位于东交民巷内，由英、法、美、德、日、俄六国于1905年合资建成。饭店采用三层砖石结构，是当时北京最高的洋楼之一，有客房两百余套，内部配备电话、电梯、暖气、自来水、卫生间等现代化设施。这座饭店对北京的西式饮食和娱乐方式起到了引领作用，成为北京当时最重要的社交舞台之一，各种政治人物在此频繁活动。

逐渐兴起的近代交通
ASCENDANT MODERN TRANSPORTATION

四

京汉火车站
Hankou-Beijing Railway Station

京汉火车站与京奉火车站

19世纪末，中国启动铁路建设，时至20世纪初，在正阳门外东西两侧已各建有一个火车站。西侧是1902年建成的京汉正阳门西车站，是京汉铁路汉口至北京的北端点。东侧是1906年建成的京奉正阳门东车站，俗称"前门火车站"，是京奉铁路北京至奉天（今沈阳）的南起点。随着京奉线、京汉线、京张线等多条铁路陆续建成，北京逐渐成为全国铁路的交通枢纽。

京奉火车站
Beijing-Fengtian Railway Station

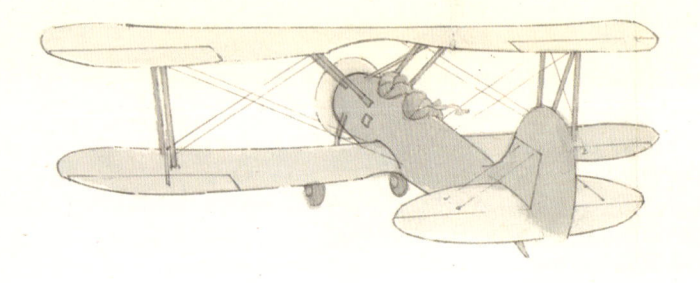

Railway Stations

China's railway construction dates back to the late 1800s. Two railway stations had been set up on the east and west flanks south of Zhengyangmen Gate. One was Zhengyangmen West Station, the terminus of the Hankou-Beijing Railway, which was completed in 1902. The other was Zhengyangmen East Station (commonly known as Qianmen Railway Station), the departure station of the Beijing-Fengtian (modern Shenyang) Railway, which was put into operation in 1906. As the railways connecting Beijing to destinations like Hankou, Fengtian, Zhangjiakou, and so on were gradually put into use, the city grew into a national rail transportation hub.

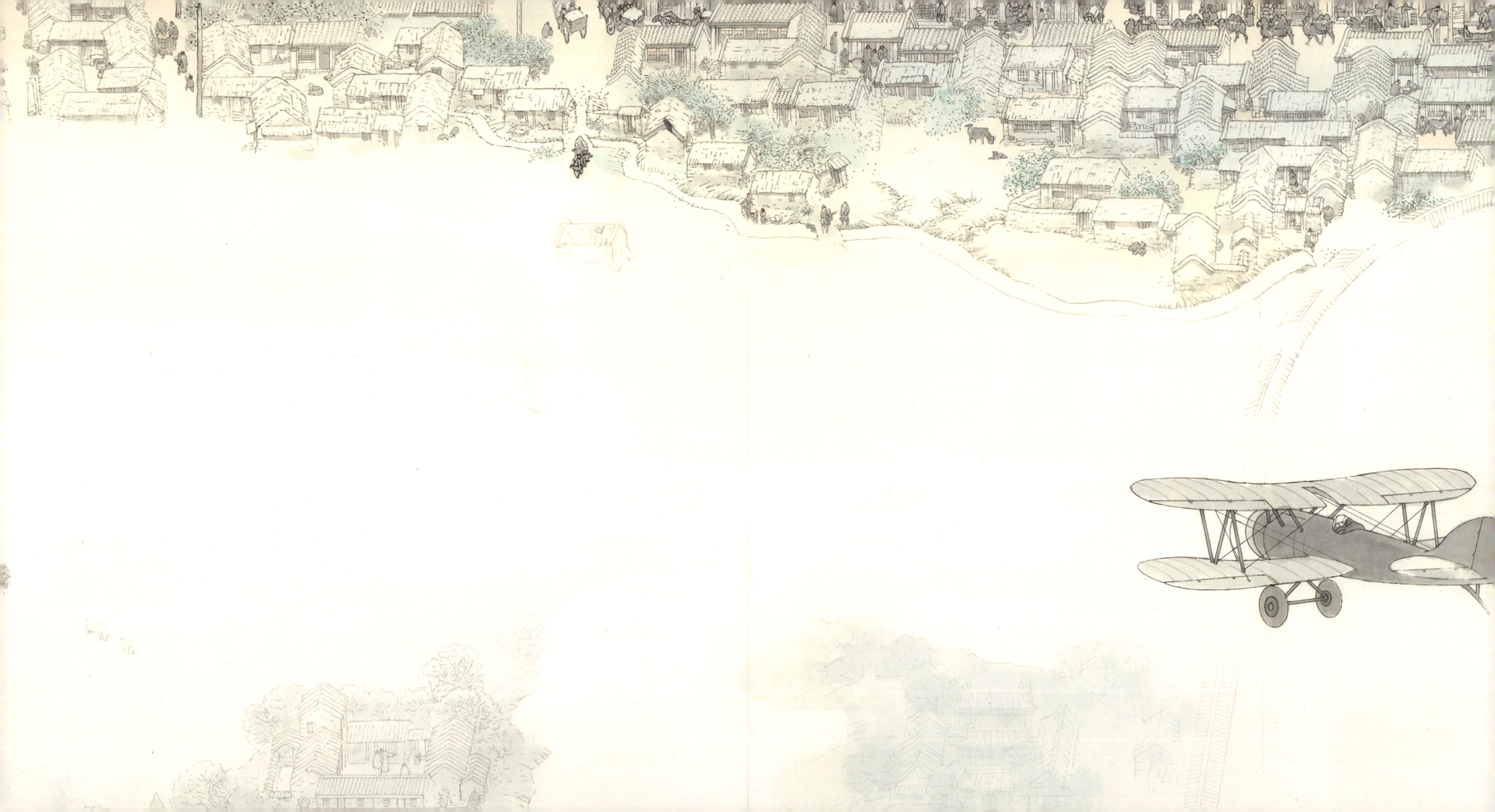

Aviation

During the startup period of China's aviation industry in 1910, a plane was purchased from France by the Qing authority. This French biplane was the first ever aircraft in China. In addition to that, the royal hunting grounds in the southern suburbs of Beijing was transformed into the Nanyuan Airport for take-offs and landings. Since then, people in Beijing began to catch sight of planes streaking across the sky every now and then. In February, 1920, the Beijing Aviation Administration was established. Two years later, the Beijing-Shanghai flight route was opened, followed by other airline routes from Beijing to destination like Nanjing, Luoyang, and so on.

航空

1910年，为筹办航空事业，清政府从法国购入中国历史上的第一架飞机——法式双翼飞机，并将位于北京南郊的皇家狩猎场改建为南苑机场以供飞机起降。从此，北京市民不时就能看到飞机从天空掠过的场景。1920年2月北京航空署成立，1922年开辟北京至上海航线，之后陆续开辟了北京至南京、北京至洛阳等地的航线。

The Railway Loop Line

Prepared and built by the newly established Beijing Municipal Office, the railway that looped around the Inner City of Beijing were put into service on the New Year's Day of 1916. It started from the Xizhimen Railway Station, which was the departure station of the Beijing-Zhangjiakou Railway, and met with the Beijing-Fengtian Railway line. Thanks to this Loop Line, transport around the city was substantially facilitated.

环城铁路

京都市政公所建立之后，开始筹划修筑环城铁路，1916年1月1日环城铁路正式通车。环城铁路所环之城为北京内城，起点为西直门，并与京张铁路、京奉铁路接轨，而西直门站又是京张铁路的起始站。环城铁路的修建给北京城的运输带来较大便利。

環城鐵路

106

Various Means of Transportation

During the late Qing and early Republic of China periods, the expansion of the urban scale and the increase in personnel travels enriched the means of transportation within Beijing. Here is a description of what he saw in 1918 by Li Dazhao, the revolutionist: "I was astonished by the scene at the often-visited Qianmen thoroughfare: How can so many vehicles of different times be fitted into such a narrow road? There you can find caravans, wheelbarrows, mule- or horse-drawn carriages, rickshaws, bicycles, cars, etc. Things which had not been invented until the 20th century were seen together with those already existed in the 15th century."

丰富的市内交通

清末民初，随着城市规模扩大，人口流动性增加，人们出行的交通方式变得多样，各种交通工具也开始在北京城内并行。革命家李大钊曾这样描述1918年左右自己看到的前门景象："我常走在前门一带通衢，觉得那样狭隘的一条道路，其间竟能容纳数多时代的器物：有骆驼轿，有一轮车，还有骡车、马车、人力车、自转车、汽车等，把20世纪的东西同15世纪以前的汇在一处。"

Automobile

Automobiles were introduced to Beijing in the late Qing Dynasty. In 1907, the Beijing-Paris World Rally Championship was hosted in the Capital City. That was quite a big event in the car race history. It required participants to set off from Deshengmen Gate and go all the way across the Eurasian continent, which was considered an unparalleled feat by the rest of the world. In 1908, a businessman attempted to apply for a business license for passenger transportation by car in the capital, but was denied. In 1913, the city's first car rental firm emerged. Since cars were relatively new to China then, the absence of traffic regulations created so many chaos and the condition lasted until 1934 when the Nationalist Government advocated the "new life campaign", in which unified traffic rules were legislated.

Bicycle

In the late Qing Dynasty and the early Republic of China, bicycles were introduced from Japan and became an important means of transportation for urban youths in modern times.

Rickshaw

In the early years of the Republic of China, rickshaws were an important means of transportation for Beijing citizens and an important means of living for the grassroots. According to statistics, there were 20,674 rickshaws in Beijing in 1917. The number increased to 37,036 in 1939. The huge population of rickshaw pullers had gradually developed into a sizable social class. They had transformed the demography and social structure of Beijing by endeavoring to play their parts in urban life.

⊙ 汽车

汽车在清末就已传入北京。1907年，北京举办了早期世界汽车赛中重要赛事——北京至巴黎的汽车拉力赛，参赛汽车从德胜门出发，横跨欧亚大陆，被"各国视为奇观"。1908年，已有商人呈请在京师开办市内汽车载客业务，但未获批准。1913年，北京出现了第一家小型出租汽车行。汽车刚刚进入中国时，还没有统一的行驶规则，时常导致交通混乱，直到1934年，国民政府推行"新生活运动"时，才特意统一了交通规则。

⊙ 自行车

清末民初，自行车从日本传入，成为都市摩登青年的重要交通工具。

⊙ 人力车

民国初年，人力车是北京市民出行的重要代步工具，也是底层民众重要的谋生手段。据统计，北京1917年就有人力车20674辆，到1939年增加到37036辆。从事人力车工作的人口逐渐发展壮大，形成了一个数量庞大的职业群体和社会阶层，在一定程度上改变了北京城的人口结构与社会结构，并在城市生活中彰显了自身的力量。

接轨国际的城市设施
UNIVERSAL URBAN FACILITIES
(五)

Telegraph Office

China's modern telecommunications industry began in the late Qing Dynasty. In 1877, the first ever Chinese telegram was sent by Li Hongzhang. In 1884, telegraph offices were set up in the Inner and Outer Cities of Beijing for official and civil uses respectively. In 1908, the Qing authority nationalized the telecommunications industry and began to plan and build telegraph networks nationwide. The crisscrossing telegraph lines at that time covered most major Chinese cities, with additional cables linking abroad. The establishment of telegraph offices and the rapid development of the telegraph services gave rise to China's telecommunications industry.

电报局

中国的电信事业开始于清末。1877年，李鸿章在天津发出了中国第一封电报。1884年，北京内外城分设了官商两处电报局，供政府和商民使用。1908年，清政府将全国电报事业收归国有，开始有规划铺设全国电报网。清末电报线路已"纵横全国，经纬相维"，除国内线路外，还开通了国外的线路。电报局的设置及电报业的迅速发展，使中国的电信事业步入国际化轨道。

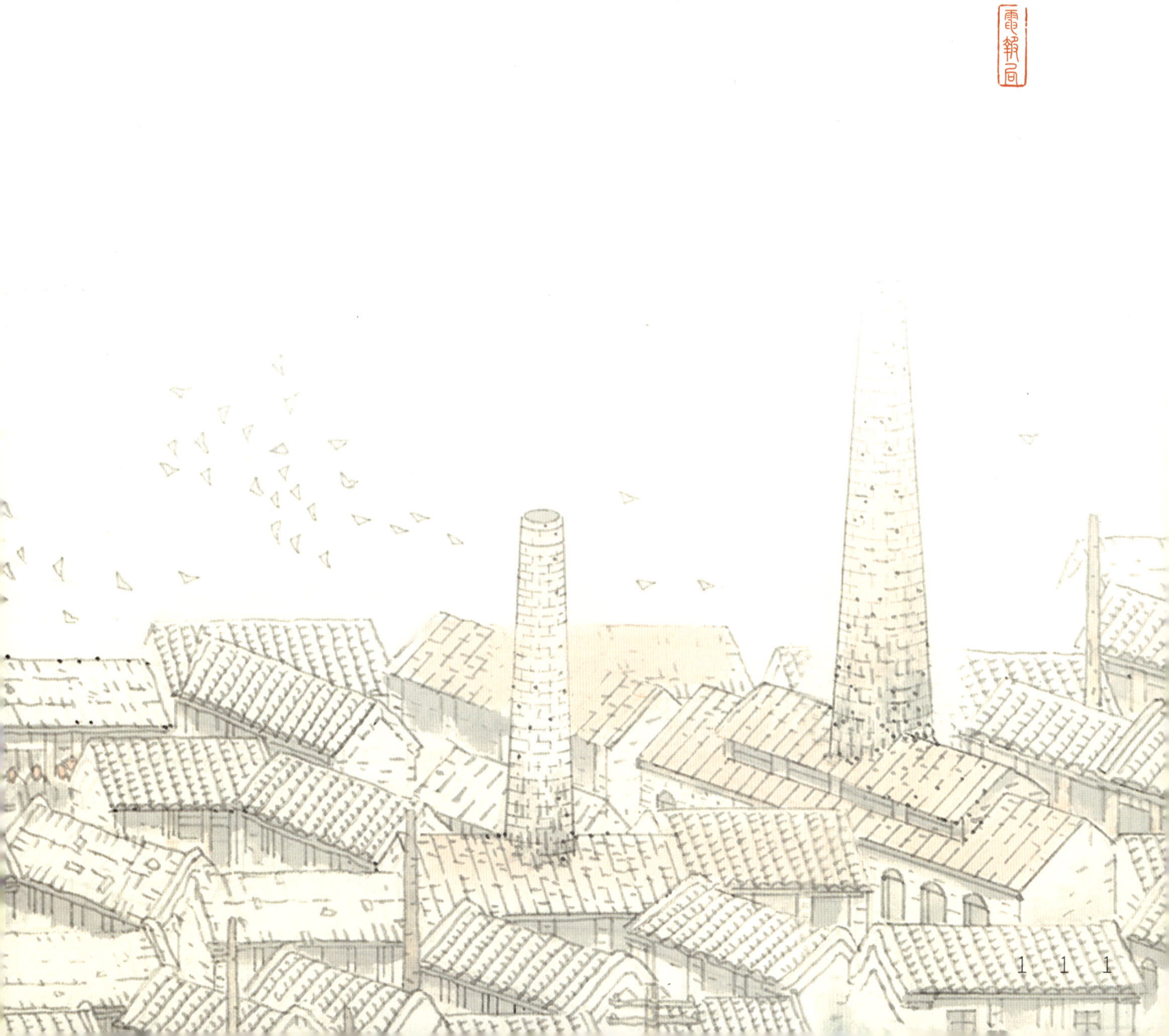
電報局

Electric Power

In 1888, the Empress Dowager Cixi introduced electricity to Beijing by ordering the installation of electric lights in her sleeping chamber at the Sea Palaces. The Legation Quarter followed suit. Things got changed in 1906 when the city's earliest power plant for civil use, co-founded by Chinese businessmen, went into operation. The Peking Chinese Electric Light & Power Co., Ltd. had electric streetlights installed on the bustling commercial zones such as Chang'an Avenue, Dongsi Shitiao *hutong*, Xisi Shitiao *hutong*, Qianmen Street, and Chongwenmen Gate. Before that, streets and alleyways were mostly lit by kerosene lamps. By 1939, a considerable proportion of the main roads in Beijing had been illuminated by electric streetlights.

京师华商电厂
Peking Chinese Electric Light & Power Co., Ltd

电力照明

　　1888年，慈禧太后在中南海寝宫仪鸾殿安装了电灯，随后，东交民巷使馆区也开始使用电灯照明。1906年，由华商筹办的京师华商电厂建成，这是北京首家发电厂。其后，电力公司陆续在东西长安街、西四、东四、前门、崇文门等繁华商业街安装电灯，取代了之前的煤油灯照明，而一些街巷胡同也陆续安装了电灯。至1939年，北京主要街道都实现了电力照明。

自来水厂

Drinking Water

Beijing's first waterwork was set up in 1908 by the Qing authority. To raise startup funding, the company went public, but was so, by order of the authority, exclusively for Chinese investors in the cause of protecting national industries. When the water plant was completed in 1910, one of its two branches at Dongzhimen Gate purified water pumped from the Sunhe River before supplying tap water to the Capital City. The tap water system was revolutionary to the traditional manual mode of water supply in Beijing, seen as a potent symbol of its citizens embracing modern lifestyle.

饮用自来水

1908年，清政府批准建立北京第一座自来水厂——京师自来水公司，选址在东直门外。自来水厂采取招商集股的方式筹集资金，为保护民族实业，政府规定只接受本国民众入股。1910年，自来水厂建成，厂址分为孙河和东直门两处，取孙河水净化后，再用水泵输送到东直门，然后向京城内居民供水。自来水供水系统的出现，改变了北京城传统的由人工运送饮水的供水方式，是北京市民生活步入近代化的有力见证。

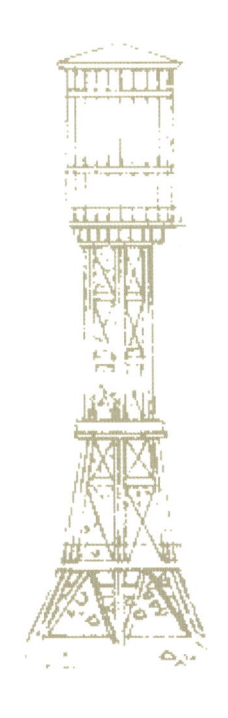

Commercial Banks

Towards the late Qing Dynasty, numerous foreign banks were found at the Legation Quarter while big local banks emerged at Xijiaominxiang *hutong*. In August, 1905, China's earliest government-owned bank run by the Ministry of Revenue was set up. It later became the Bank of the Qing Empire in 1908, functioning as both the central and commercial banks. During the Republic of China period, the Bank of the Qing Empire was reorganized as the Bank of China, with foreign exchanges as its major business. There were more than a dozen local banks around, including the Central Bank, the Industrial Bank of China, the Agricultural Bank of China, and the Mainland Bank. The emergence of banks from both home and abroad in Beijing not only brought in new concepts and forms in finance, but also contributed to the booming of China's financial industry.

西交民巷
Xijiaominxiang *hutong*

商业银行

清朝末年,北京开始出现了一大批商业银行。其中,东交民巷一带外国银行林立,而西交民巷一带则是众多中国本土银行的聚集地。1905年8月,中国首家官办银行户部银行设立,1908年改名大清银行,兼具中央金融机构与商业银行的双重职能。到了民国时期,大清银行被改组为中国银行,主要经营外汇。西交民巷又有中央银行、中国实业银行、中国农业银行、大陆银行等十多家本土银行。北京这些中外银行的出现,一方面吸取了国外新的金融理念及形式;另一方面,促进了中国金融业的发展和繁荣。

Westernized Hospitals

Since modern times, foreign missionaries not only brought along with them Western religions but also introduced Western medicine and advanced medical equipment. China's modern healthcare services today can be traced to the late Qing and early Republic of China periods, when Westernized hospitals sponsored by either domestic or overseas funds were established in Beijing.

西式医院

自近代以来，外国传教士除了传播宗教信仰，还将西方医学和新的医疗设备带来中国。清末民初，北京城中已经有了一些中国人和外国人创办的西式医院，这些医院开启了中国的近现代医疗并延续至今。

协和医院
Peking Union Medical College Hospital

⊙ **Hopkins Memorial Hospital**

　　Founded in 1903, Hopkins Memorial Hospital was formerly an eye clinic sponsored by the Methodist Episcopal Church from the United States. In 1906, optical service became available in the hospital, therefore the history of Chinese people having to travel abroad for the right prescription glasses drew to an end. Today it is called Beijing Tongren Hospital.

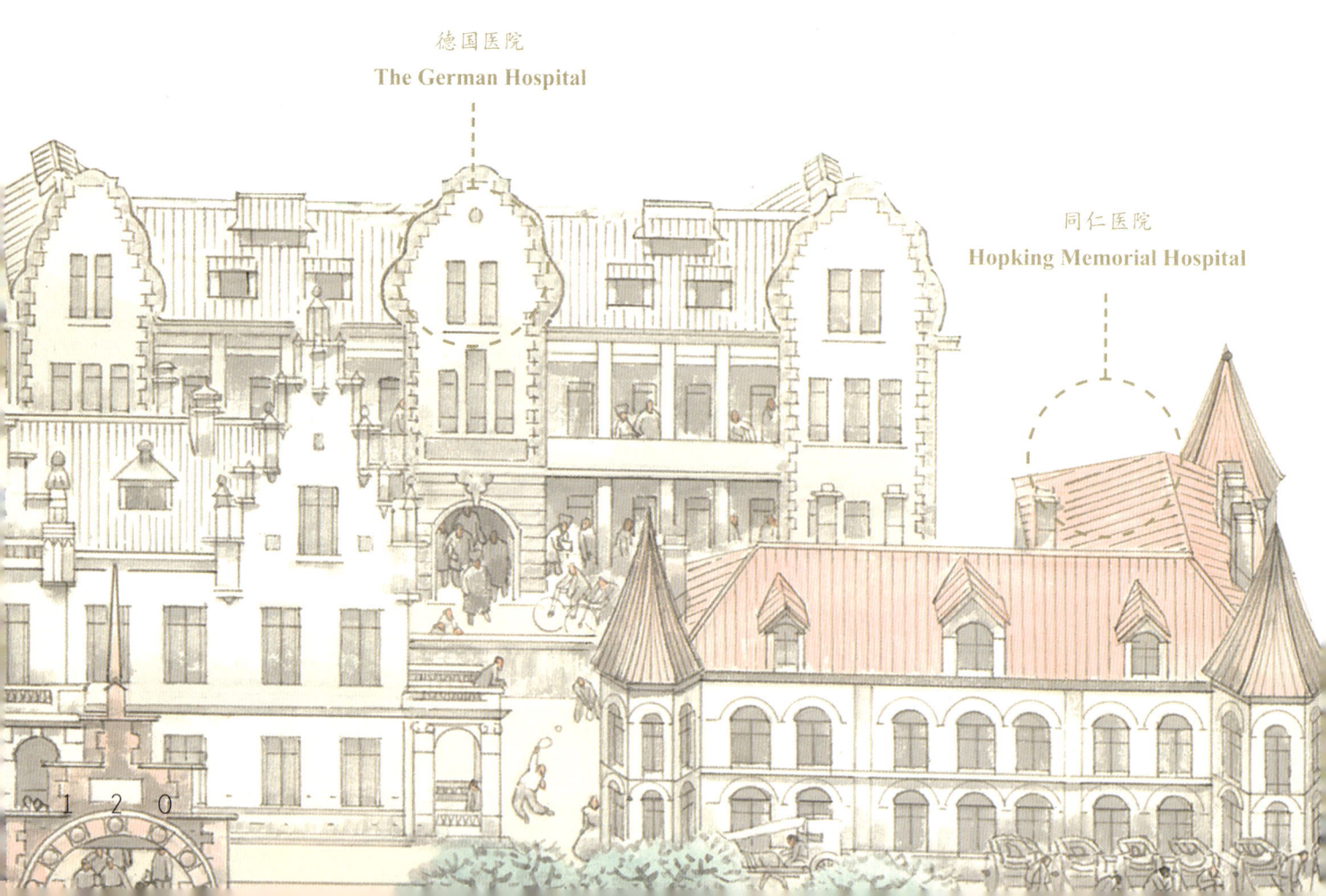

德国医院
The German Hospital

同仁医院
Hopking Memorial Hospital

⊙ **The German Hospital**

The German Hospital founded in 1905 at the Legation Quarter was built by the German government with some of the Boxer Indemnity paid by China. It is the predecessor of the present-day Beijing Hospital.

⊙ **Peking Union Medical College Hospital**

Peking Union Medical College Hospital was founded in 1921 by the Rockefeller Foundation based in the United States, functioning as both a hospital and a medical school.

⊙ 同仁医院

创建于1903年的同仁医院，其前身是美国美以美教会开办的眼科诊所，1906年医院成立磨镜室，结束了国人需要到国外才能配眼镜的历史。现在为北京同仁医院。

⊙ 德国医院

创建于1905年的德国医院，即今天的北京医院。当时是德国政府用部分庚子赔款在使馆区为外国使团建立的医院。

⊙ 协和医院

创建于1921年的协和医院，是美国洛克菲勒基金会投资创办，在治病救人的同时，也创办了医学堂培养医学人才。

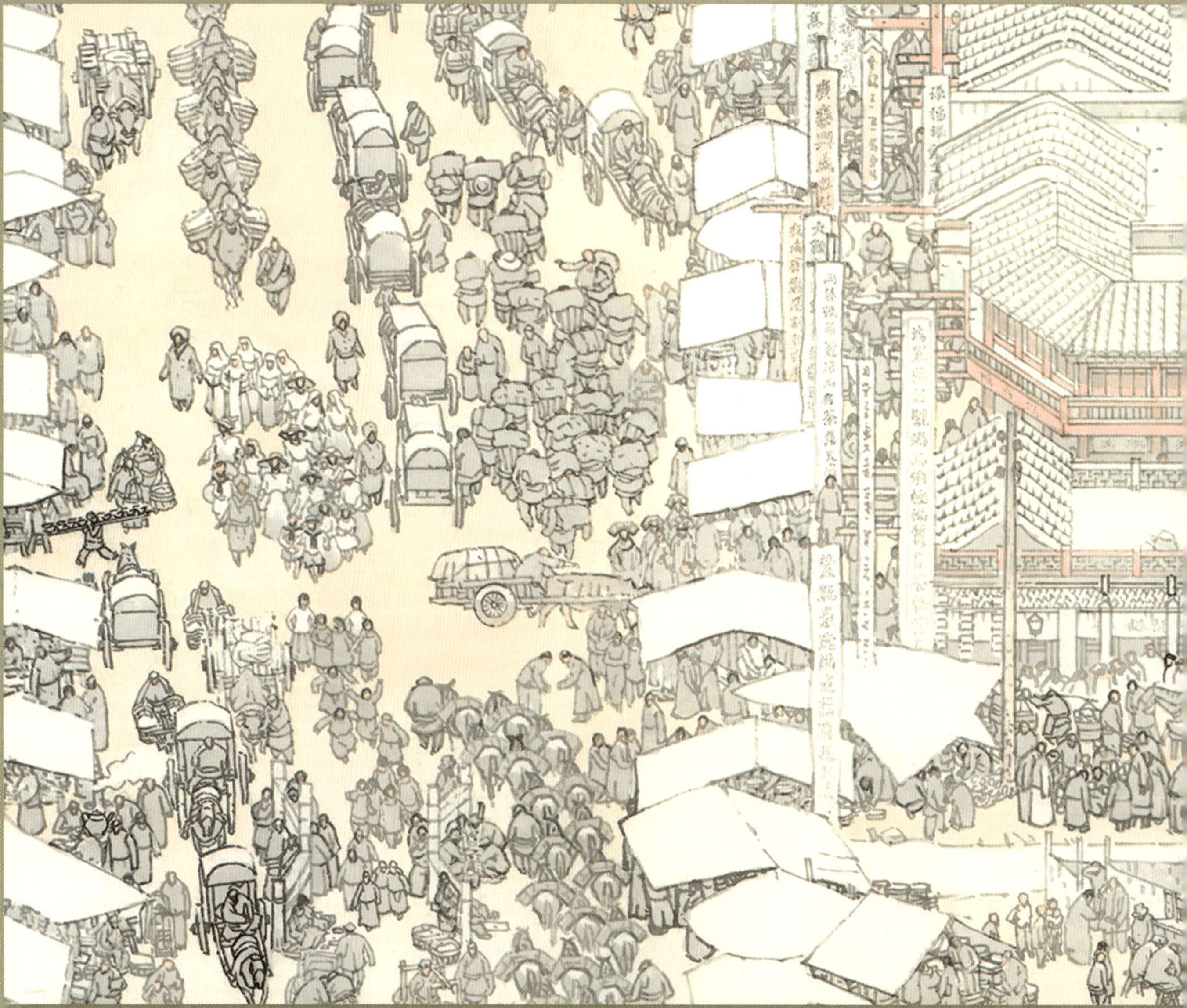

第三章 市民生活
CHAPTER 3 LIFE OF CITIZENS

Changes in the political regime have brought along transformations in urban configuration and functions. The fall of the Qing empire gave rise to the public domain as well as the modern industries and commerce, injecting vitality to this historical city.

To the south of the three southern gates of the Inner City, traditional business districts were bustling as always. Qianmen Street, Bada *hutong*, Liulichang Bookfair, and Tianqiao Market were crowded with businesses. The newly established pilot commercial block of Xiangchang was equipped with modernized urban infrastructures and recreational sites, bringing new lifestyles to those living in the southern part of Beijing.

Due to its proximity to the Legation Quarter, Wangfujing Street became the city's most prosperous hotspot in terms of commerce and trade. Its high-end and fashionable profile was significantly different from Beijing's business presence before.

Civic culture developed rapidly: on one hand, the former residence of the nobles and patricians gradually became part of the alleyways (*hutong*) where ordinary people dwelled in. On the other hand, the Forbidden City, a unique symbol of the imperial family, was turned into the Palace Museum opened to the public. People held various beliefs, so there were different types of religious constructions scattered around the city where different customs and cultures met.

政体的变更带来的是城市形态与功能的转变。当皇权消失，公共领域逐渐拓展，近代工商业兴起，这座历史悠久的古城内居住的民众开始焕发出新的生机。

"前三门"外，传统的南城商业区依然人声鼎沸、喧闹繁华。前门商业区、八大胡同、琉璃厂旧书肆、天桥地摊无不延续着昔日的繁荣景象；香厂新市区新式建筑、综合性商场、娱乐场所林立，全新的城市设施丰富了城南地区的市民生活。

内城的新式商业空间也在兴起，地处显贵之地且毗邻使馆区的王府井大街一带，成为北京商贸最为繁华的区域，其富丽堂皇、洋气十足的特点与北京传统商业面貌呈现出较大差异。

代表贵族的王府宅门逐渐融入平民的胡同，代表皇室的紫禁城变成了市民随意参观的博物馆，市民文化迅速发展起来。市民阶层仍然保持着丰富的民间信仰，不同类型的宗教建筑分布于城内，不同习俗与文化在北京城中交融。

焕然一新的商业街区

FRESHENED COMMERCIAL BLOCKS

一

Wangfujing Street

Located east of Donghuamen Gate, Wangfujing Street (a.k.a. Morrison Street by expatriates in Beijing previously) has been one of the most renown commercial blocks in Beijing. Being a vital passage of the Imperial City, commerce also began to thrive in its immediate area since the gradual deregulation of trade within the Inner City during the late Qing Dynasty. In 1914, municipal renovation projects began at Wangfujing Street. Its traffic convenience attracted many foreign firms and shops to start business here, turning the place into the most flourishing business area in Beijing. Wangfujing Street was more like a metropolis of upscale Westernized styles compared to the other traditional business districts in Beijing: world-renowned brands as well as everything from soup to nuts could easily be found here, including automobiles, timepieces, electrical appliances, diamonds, business suits, etc.

Scan QR code for VR experience

王府井大街

王府井大街，位于东华门外，是北京最著名的商业街区之一。由于地处皇城的重要通道，在清后期，内城不得经商的禁令逐渐松弛后，王府井地区商业属性开始凸显。1914年，王府井大街开始道路改造工程，便利的交通吸引了一大批高档洋行、商铺纷纷进驻，成为北京商贸最为繁荣的区域。国际大牌在这里随处可见，汽车、钟表、电器、钻石、西装等在这里应有尽有，王府井大街所呈现出的这种高端消费、西方风格等独特气象，与北京传统商业区形成明显差异。

扫码观看现在的王府井大街

王府井大街

Dong'an Market

Dong'an Market was seated at the northern tip of Wangfujing Street. During the municipal constructions in the late Qing Dynasty, shops and stalls east of Dong'anmen Gate were relocated and a fixed marketplace was consequentially formed. Dong'an Market was the earliest regular bazaar organized by the authority, providing locals with all sorts of daily necessities, foods, and entertainment, as well as theaters, teahouses, and cinemas. The prosperity of Dong'an Market made Wangfujing Street even more flourishing.

东安市场

　　东安市场位于王府井大街北端。清朝末年，为推行近代市政，清政府将东安门外店铺、商摊全部迁至这里营业，逐渐形成了固定的商业场所。东安市场是北京城最早由官方设立的综合型定期集市，其经营范围覆盖了日用百货、饮食、娱乐等众多与市民日常生活相关的商品，还出现了一批戏院、茶馆、影院等休闲娱乐场所。东安市场的繁荣也带动了王府井商业街的进一步繁荣。

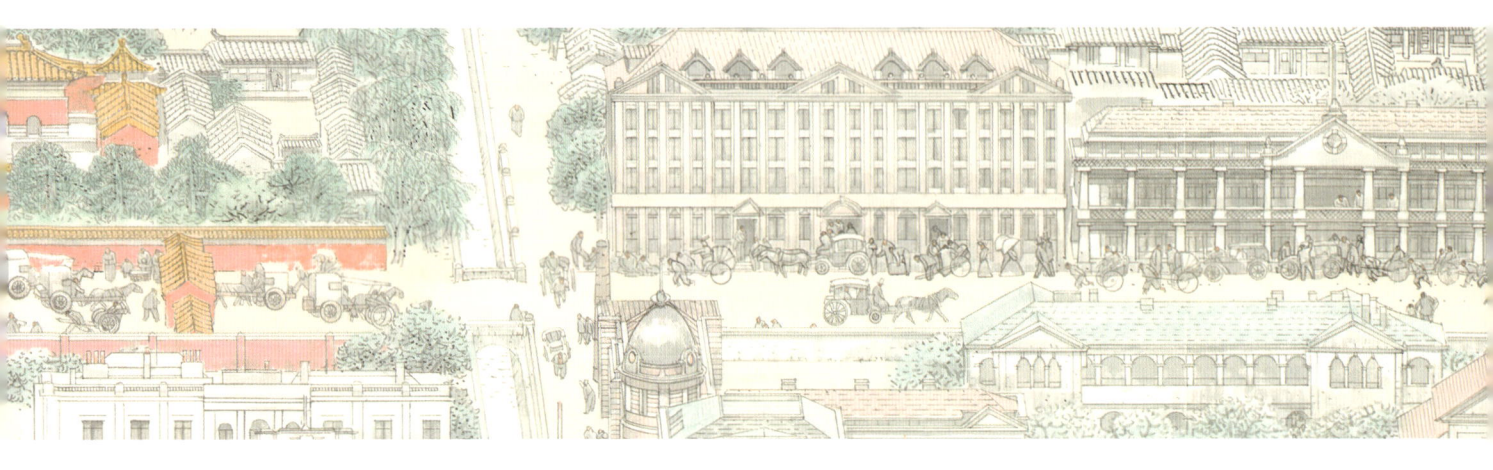

East Chang'an Avenue (The Long Peace Street, East)

East Chang'an Avenue (The Long Peace Street) of the late 1800s and early 1900s was quite different from what we see today. At that time, the east and west sections of today's Chang'an Avenue was cut off by an enclosure in front of Tian'anmen. The thoroughfare in between the Left Chang'an Gate (the Eastern Long Peace Gate) and Dongdan *pailou* (the eastern archway) was called the East Chang'an Avenue. Together with the nearby Wangfujing Street, it was among the earliest urbanized areas in Beijing. Without malls or hurrying people, the East Chang'an Avenue was typical of the ease and leisure of a modern city. Thanks to the municipal renovation project, the avenue looked spacious and particularly clean. Pedestrians and vehicles were seen come and go along the wide asphalt road, which would be illuminated by electric lights at night. Rows of Western-style buildings lined the street; men and women, either from home or abroad, were seen strolling down the boulevard.

东长安街

　　清末民初，长安街和今天有很大不同。当时天安门前是一个封闭区域，东西两侧分别是长安左门与长安右门。从长安左门至东单牌楼一段就是当时的东长安街，与王府井大街毗邻，也是北京最早开始城市化进程的区域之一。没有偌大的商店，没有疲惫的奔忙，东长安街展现出了都市的安逸与闲适。道路改造工程后，东长安街街道宽阔，整洁异常。行人和车辆在宽阔的沥青路上来来往往，夜间有路灯照明，街边近代化建筑鳞次栉比，常常有本国或异国的男男女女在人行道树荫下散步闲逛。

北京飯店

Beijing Hotel

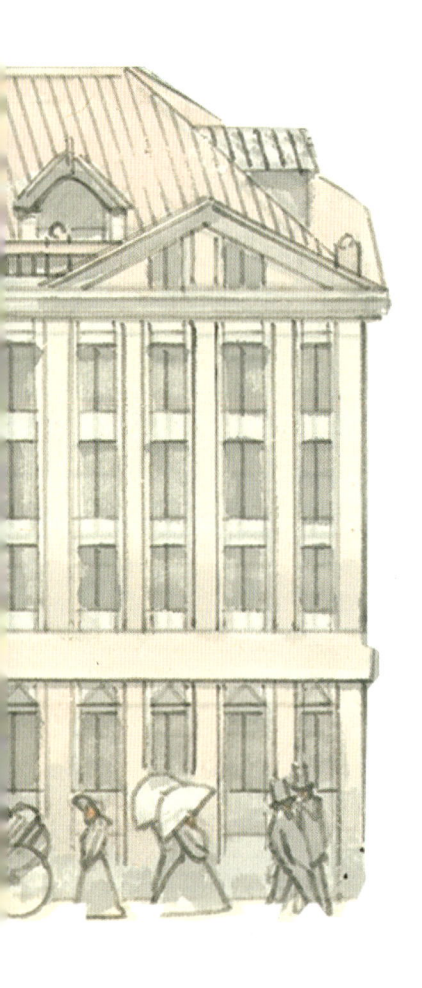

Beijing Hotel was located at the south entrance of Wangfujing Street. In 1907, the original hotel was sold to the Sino-France Industrial Bank who had the five-story upscale Grand Hôtel de Pékin completed. In 1917, a seven-story west wing of Beaux-Arts style was added. On its guest list during the years of the Republic of China were influential figures like Sun Yat-sen, Feng Yuxiang, Zhang Xueliang, etc. The founding banquet of the People's Republic of China was also held there.

北京饭店

北京饭店位于王府井大街南口，1907年由中法实业银行接手，建成了五层高档饭店，1917年又在西侧建起七层法式楼房。民国时期，北京饭店接待过孙中山、冯玉祥、张学良等风云人物。中华人民共和国成立时，开国大典宴会就在这里举办，很多重要活动也是在这里举行的。

Xiangchang New District

Xiangchang was located in the Outer City and made prosperous by temple fairs during the late Qing Dynasty. In 1914, the place was chosen as a pilot community for the urban renewal program and renamed Xiangchang New District thereafter. Unified planning was adopted by the Beijing Municipal Office, as a result of which roads and pavements were built, electric wires, telephone lines, water pipes, and underground drainage pipelines laid, and Western-style architectures built, including the New World Shopping Mall, Chengnan Amusement Park, and the Oriental Hotel. After several years of effort, Xiangchang New District had gradually grown into a cutting-edge urban community integrating commerce, entertainment, and catering. Again, it was considered a model pattern for public-private partnership in terms of promoting the urbanization process.

香厂新市区

香厂地区位于外城,清末因庙会而兴盛。1914年,香厂被选为"模范市区"建设示范区,命名为"香厂新市区"。京都市政公所对香厂一带采取统一规划——修筑道路、改造地面、铺设电线、电话线、自来水管、地下排水管线等,同时兴建了一些新式建筑,如新世界商场、城南游艺园、东方饭店等。经过几年建设,香厂逐渐成为集商业、娱乐、餐饮等于一体的新型城市街区,也成为政府与市场共同推进城市化进程的典范。

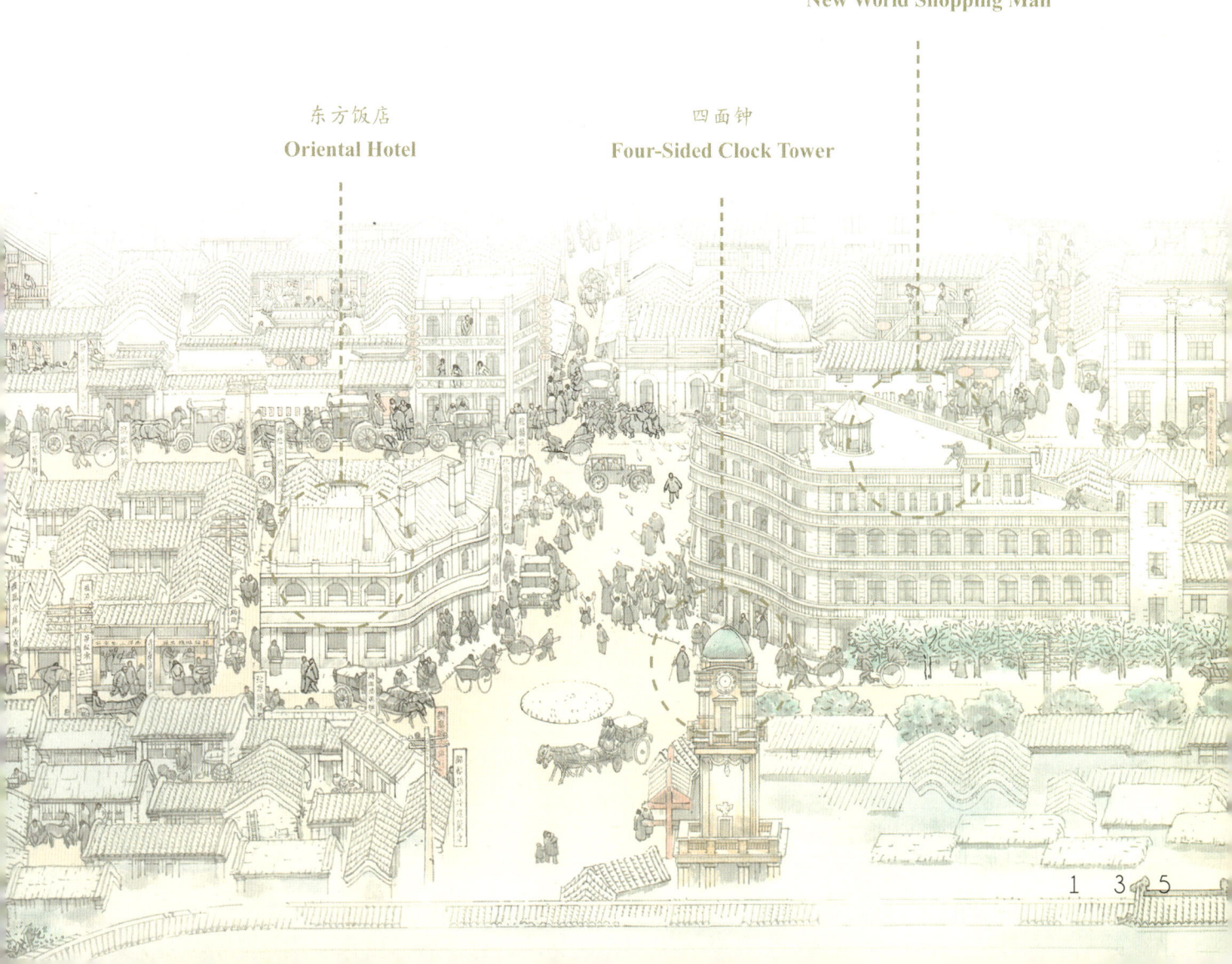

新世界商场
New World Shopping Mall

东方饭店
Oriental Hotel

四面钟
Four-Sided Clock Tower

New World Shopping Mall

Modeled after Shanghai Big World Amusement Park and designed with a giant ship outline, Beijing's New World Shopping Mall was once a landmark of Xiangchang New District. As the city's largest and most advanced indoor commercial complex of the day, its opening ceremony during the Spring Festival of 1918 even caused a sensation in Beijing. Here, people could not only do the shopping, but also go to cinemas, acrobatic performances, and various restaurants, teahouses, cafes, etc. Such a comprehensive venue integrating entertainment, catering, and shopping experience was absolutely new and trendy to the city.

新世界商场

新世界商场是香厂新市区的标志性建筑。整栋建筑仿照上海大世界游艺场建造，形似轮船，是当时京城规模最大、设施最先进的室内综合商业场所。1918年春节，新世界商场开业，轰动京城。商场内不仅可以购物，还设有电影院、杂耍场、各色菜馆、茶屋、咖啡厅等餐饮、娱乐场所。这种集娱乐、餐饮及购物于一体的商场，在当时的京城是一种新生事物，引领了时尚的新潮流。

新世界商場

Chengnan Amusement Park

Chengnan Amusement Park was opened for business on February 1, 1919. It was located near the northern part of the Altar of Agriculture, less than one kilometer away from the New World Shopping Mall. Chengnan Amusement Park was a comprehensive entertainment venue offering Peking Opera and modern drama shows, movies, and acrobatic performances, as well as games such as billiards, bowling, and roller skating. Affordable admission fees there made it the premium recreational site in the southern part of Beijing.

城南游艺园

1919年2月1日，城南游艺园在距离新世界商场不足一公里的先农坛外坛北部建成开业。作为当时的综合娱乐场所，城南游艺园不仅有京剧、文明戏、电影、杂耍等演出场所，还有台球、保龄球、旱冰等娱乐场所。由于入园票价低廉，很适合普通市民消费，所以城南游艺园成为南城首屈一指的商业娱乐中心。

⊙ The Four-Sided Clock Tower

Within reach of Chengnan Amusement Park there was a landmark construction over ten meters high called the Four-sided Clock Tower. It was said that the boss of the Amusement Park played a trick by superstitiously sabotaging the business of his rival. He believed the vessel-like New World Shopping Mall could no longer sail towards wealth once hindered by this anchor-shaped clock tower. But as the national capital was moved south, both the New World Shopping Mall and Chengnan Amusement Park suffered a disastrous decline in business. The former was put to other uses, while the latter ironically became a slaughterhouse. The once booming southern part of Beijing became the city's vaguely remembered past.

⊙ 四面钟

四面钟是城南游艺园的标志性建筑，高十几米，形状像一根铁锚。相传，建造者是要用这只铁锚拴住新世界商场这艘"轮船"，使它无法向"钱"（前）开。然而，随着国民政府南迁，新世界和城南游艺园的生意都一落千丈。新世界游艺场楼房挪作他用，城南游艺园还一度成了屠宰场。昔日的城南盛景也就渐渐淡出了人们的记忆。

140

The Oriental Hotel

The Oriental Hotel stood opposite the New World Shopping Mall. Financed and built by the Chinese, this modernized hotel went into business in February, 1918. In those years, it was regarded as one of the three most luxury hotels in Beijing together with Beijing Hotel and Grand Hotel des Wagons-Lits. The Oriental Hotel was a Western-style building with guestrooms paved with solid wooden floors and equipped with electric lights, fans, heating, and imported flush toilets. Even more amazing was that out of the 45 automobiles registered in Beijing for civilian use in 1918, seven were registered under the Oriental Hotel for the exclusive use of its stay-in guests. Celebrities on its guestlist included Li Dazhao, Chen Duxiu, Cai Yuanpei, Zhang Xueliang, Bai Chongxi, and Hu Shi.

东方饭店

东方饭店坐落在新世界商场的斜对面，是中国人筹资兴建的现代化饭店。1918年2月开始营业，与北京饭店、六国饭店并称为当时北京三大高档饭店。东方饭店是西式建筑，客房全部采用实木地板，配有电灯、电扇、暖气和进口的抽水马桶等。更令人惊奇的是，1918年在北京登记的四十五辆民用车中，有七辆是属于东方饭店的，供住店贵宾使用。当时，包括李大钊、陈独秀、蔡元培、张学良、白崇禧、胡适在内的社会名流都曾下榻过东方饭店。

Qianmen Street

The thoroughfare south of Zhengyangmen Gate was Qianmen Street. Since commerce and entertainment within the Inner City were banned during the early years of the Qing Dynasty, those activities were only allowed in the Outer City, with Qianmen Street connecting the Inner and Outer Cities particularly vibrant in trade. On both sides of the north-south Qianmen Street, there emerged two symmetrical commercial blocks–Dashilar on the west and Xianyukou on the east. Numerous century-old brands can still be found there, such as Yueshengzhai Ma's Halal grocery, Zhangyiyuan teahouse, Tongrentang pharmacy, Refosian silk and cotton clothing shop, etc. Also abundant were restaurants, money houses, all kinds of shops selling jewelry and so on, making it a thriving trading area.

前门大街

出了正阳门就是前门大街。清代初期，由于内城不准经营商业及演艺活动，商业及演艺场所大都设置于外城。连接内外城的前门大街，商业活动尤为繁荣。而在前门大街两侧，又形成了大栅栏和鲜鱼口两个东西对称的商业街区。这里有众多传承至今的百年老字号，如月盛斋马家老铺、张一元茶庄、同仁堂药店、瑞蚨祥绸庄等。还有数不清的饭馆、酒楼，银号、钱庄、金店，各种百货商店汇集于此，使前门大街的人气旺盛，买卖兴隆。

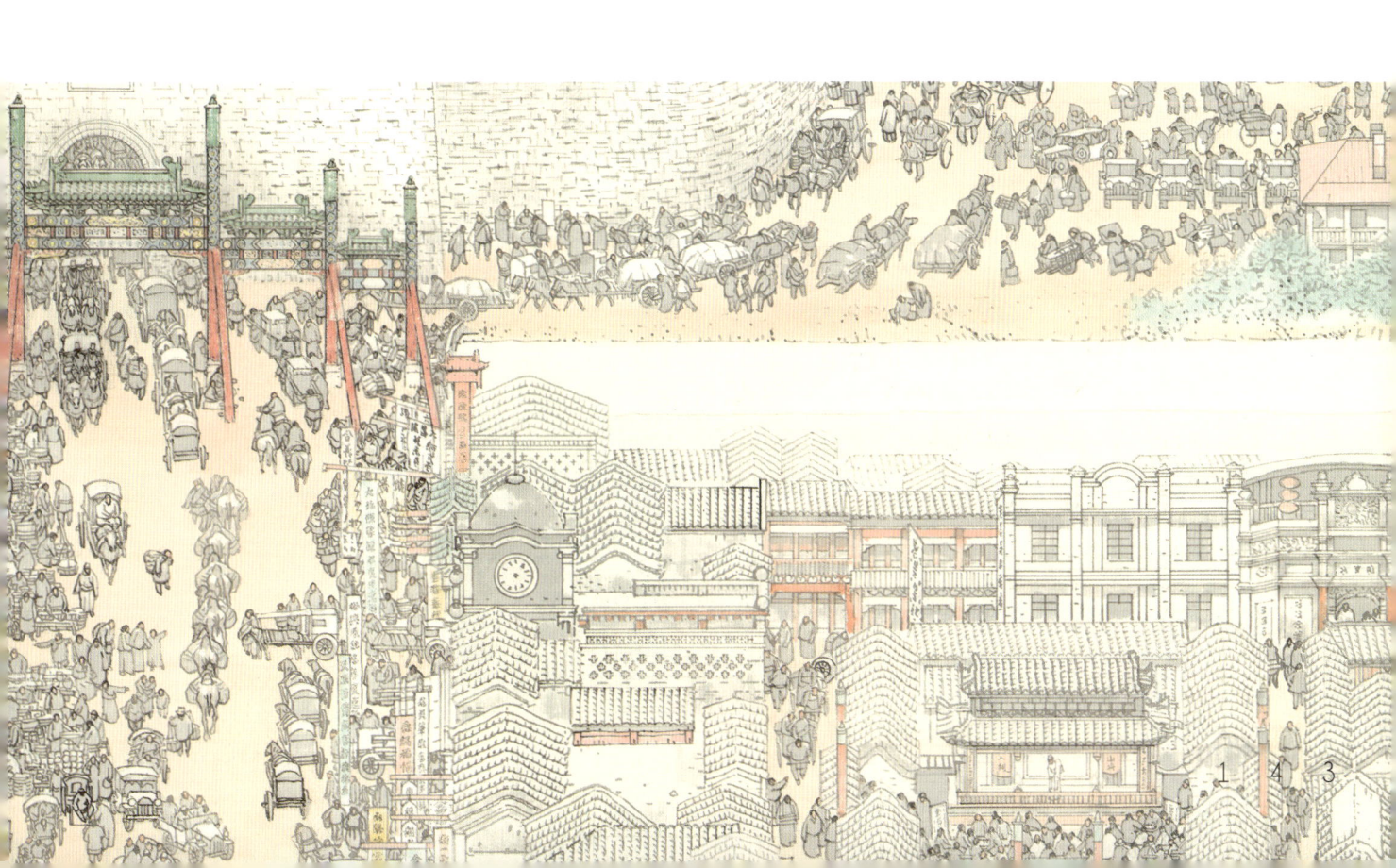

144

Bada *hutong* (The Eight Famous Alleyways)

Once a synonym for the Red Light District in Beijing, Bada *hutong* was an area west of Qianmen Street. It benefited from not only the bustling Qianmen area and many other commercial blocks nearby, but also the fact that brothels were prohibited in the Inner City, hence their relocation there. After the municipal police system was introduced, brothels and prostitutes were included in municipal management, which meant brothels were only allowed to do business in a predetermined zone set by the municipal authority. The love stories drawn from the storytelling scripts between Xiaofengxian and General Cai E were said to take place there.

八大胡同

八大胡同是当时北京城知名的风月场所，位于前门大街西侧的闹市之中，与众多商业街区毗邻。因为内城禁止设置青楼、妓院等场所，于是这些场所便在这里聚集。清末民初，北京引入市政警察体系，将妓院和娼妓正式纳入市政管理，并圈定了妓院的设置范围。在八大胡同中，最有名的当数上林仙馆，话本中广为人知的青楼女子小凤仙与蔡锷将军的爱情故事，就发生在这里。

Liulichang

Situated to the west of Dashilar and Zhushikou south of Zhengyangmen Gate, Liulichang was called by this name because it was the site of a previous imperial kiln of glazed tiles during the Ming Dynasty. It gradually developed into a culturally rich neighborhood where bookshops and book fairs were everywhere to be found, and frequently patronized by famous scholars. During the Republic of China period, bookshops at Liulichang remained a dream place for many scholars. In his fifteen years in Beijing, Lu Xun, the famous Chinese writer and revolutionist, was said to have visited the place 485 times and purchased more than 3,800 volumes of books and rubbings from stone inscriptions. Many scholars still go there in search of rare books and manuscripts even to this day.

Scan QR code for VR experience

扫码观看现在的琉璃厂

琉璃厂

琉璃厂位于正阳门外大栅栏、珠市口的西侧，明代为皇家烧制琉璃瓦件的窑厂，故得名。到了清代，这里逐渐发展为古书集市汇聚的文化街，是许多著名学者经常惠顾的场所。民国时期，琉璃厂书肆依然在众多学者心中保持着崇高的地位，著名文学家、革命家鲁迅先生在北京的十五年间，去琉璃厂的次数即多达四百八十五次，采买图书、碑帖等文献共三千八百余册。今天这里仍然是众多学者购买古籍的主要场所。

Tianqiao (The Heavenly Bridge)

Located outside Zhengyangmen Gate, Tianqiao was originally a white marble bridge built over Longxugou (the Dragon Beard Ditch) on the Central Axis. It was called by this name because, for the Ming and Qing emperors, this was the only way to and from the Temple of Heaven where they offered sacrifice. The stone bridge was demolished but its name remained. In 1914, both the barbican and marketplace by the side of the Outer City wall were dismantled for the sake of the renovation project of Zhengyangmen Gate. The originally Hebao Lane Market was relocated to an open space southwest of Tianqiao, which rapidly promoted the commercial development and traffic construction of the area, and gradually formed the unique folk culture of Tianqiao in contrast to the Imperial City culture of the Inner City.

⊙ Longxugou (Dragon Beard Ditch)

Adjacent to the Tianqiao Market was the Dragon Beard Ditch where many impoverished people lived in the dilapidated low altitude shanty towns alongside the riverbanks, areas of high flood risk.

天桥

　　天桥位于正阳门外，原是中轴线上跨越龙须沟的一座汉白玉石桥，是明清两代帝王赴天坛祭祀的必经之桥，所以被称为天桥。后石桥被拆除，地名则保留至今。1914年，为推进正阳门改造工程建设，瓮城及城脚下的荷包巷市场被拆除，迁建至天桥西南空地的平民市场，迅速推动了天桥两侧的商业发展及交通建设，并逐渐形成了与内城的皇城文化相对应的天桥民俗文化。

⊙ 龙须沟

　　天桥市场旁的龙须沟一带是当时贫苦百姓的聚居地。沿岸多为棚户，房屋低矮，四壁透风，到了下雨天，沟里的积水还会出现倒灌。

Shichahai (The Ten Temples Lakes)

Shichahai, also known as Haizi, is actually a collective name for the three lakes of Qianhai, Houhai, and Xihai, as well as their environs. Hailed as somewhere equal to the regions south of the Yangtze River in downtown Beijing by virtue of its abundant water sources, Shichahai was considered a major recreational attraction among the locals. Numerous temples, princely residences, and former residences of celebrities could be found in the vicinity. All the more invitingly attractive there are the well-planned and nicely decorated folk dwellings scattered around the lakes.

Scan QR code for VR experience

扫码观看现在的什刹海

什刹海

  什刹海指的是前海、后海和西海三片水域及周边地区，又曾称海子等。因为水系丰富，这里一直被誉为都城中的江南，是京城人士休闲游玩的主要场所。什刹海周边有众多寺观、王公府第和名人故居。格局严整又极富生活情趣的民居建筑则是什刹海的又一特色景观。

隆福寺庙会
Longfu Temple Fair

Temple Fairs

Going to temple fairs (*ganmiao*) originated from the regularly held religious fetes and later became folk festivals. In the old days, there had been a wide variety of temple fairs in Beijing. Different temple fairs had their own features according to the deities they worshipped: the Miaofeng Mountain Incense Festival and the Peach Banquet held to celebrate Wangmuniangniang (the Queen Mother)'s birthday at the Peach Palace. At Tibetan Buddhist temples like the Lama Temple, temple fairs were mainly dedicated to expelling evil spirits. Whenever there were temple fairs, sightseers, vendors, and folk artists almost blocked the temple from the inside out. As time went by, regular markets were gradually formed in the surrounding areas. In the Qing Dynasty Beijing, there were already four major temple fairs regularly held at Longfu Temple, Huguo Temple, the White Stupa Temple, and the Shrine of Gnome. Even into the early 1900s, temple fairs were still one of the most important activities for people to spend their leisure time on and have fun.

庙会

庙会源于宗教节日中的祭祀活动，俗称"赶庙"，由于定期举办，逐渐成为民俗节日。旧时北京庙会繁多，各庙会根据寺观供奉神位不同而各有特色，如妙峰山香会的争"头香"，蟠桃宫在王母娘娘寿辰开办的"蟠桃盛会"，藏传佛教寺院雍和宫的"打鬼"。每到开庙日，寺内寺外人流如织，大批小商小贩、民间艺人在寺观周边聚集，久而久之形成了定期的市集，热闹非凡。时至清代，北京已经形成了隆福寺、护国寺、白塔寺、土地庙四大定期庙会。清末民初，丰富的庙会仍然是人们重要的休闲娱乐方式。

蟠桃宫庙会
The Peach Palace Temple Fair

Public Gardens

Scan QR code for VR experience

    After the Qing Dynasty, a large number of imperial gardens and temples in Beijing were nationalized. Later the Beijing Municipal Office attempted to transform some of them into modern parks out of the Western concepts of city making. The most far-reaching cases would be the Central Park (the former Altar of Land and Grain), Chengnan Park (the former Temple of Agriculture), the Temple of Heaven Park, Beihai Park (part of the former Xiyuan), and Jingzhao Park (the former Temple of Earth) being opened to the public. Parkgoers were able to enjoy the built-in teahouses, photo studios, poolrooms, and even libraries. Parks became a public place for Beijing citizens to engage in cultural activities.

北海公园
Beihai Park

公共园林

清朝灭亡后,北京的一大批皇家园林和坛庙收归国有。本着现代城市的建设理念,京都市政公所将它们陆续改造为现代公园。其中影响较大的公园主要有:由社稷坛改建的中央公园,由先农坛改建的城南公园,由天坛改建的天坛公园,由西苑改建的北海公园,由地坛改建的京兆公园等。这些公园中通常有茶楼、照相馆、球房等娱乐场所,有些还设有阅览室等设施,成为广大市民从事文化活动的公共场所。

扫码观看现在的北海公园

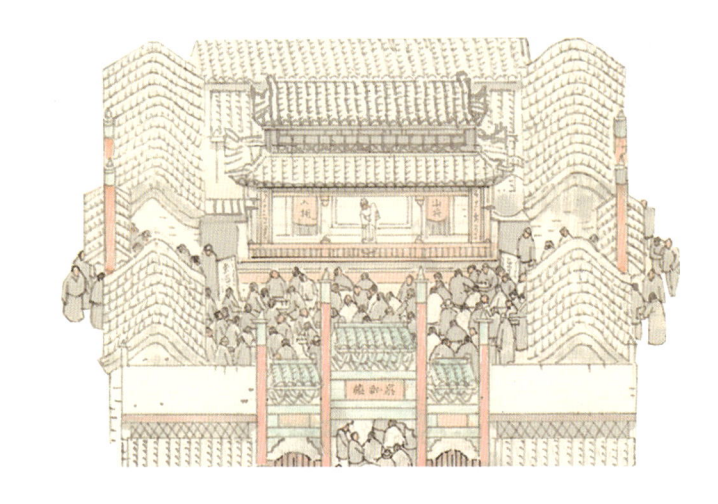

Opera Performances at Teahouses

    Watching opera performances while drinking tea has long been a typical pastime for Beijing citizens. With the growing popularity of opera performances during the late Qing and early Republic of China periods, new types of theatres emerged. Among them was the Auspicious Tea Garden opened for business in 1908. Located next to the Dong'an Market as the first of its kind, it caused a real sensation in Beijing. Later, modeled after the Grand Stage in Shanghai, the No. 1 Stage on Zhushikou Xidajie (west street) brought in a new type of theater by offering a three-story auditorium able to accommodate 3,000 audiences and with private boxes for VIP reservations on the second floor. Besides being the earliest in the capital to have night shows, Wenming Xiyuan (a teahouse with modern drama shows) near Zhushikou was also the first to receive female audiences and to have actresses on stage.

茶馆剧场

    看戏喝茶是北京市民的传统休闲娱乐活动。清末民初，随着戏曲演出市场日渐兴盛，出现了一些新式剧场。1908年，吉祥茶园在东安市场旁开张营业，成为北京第一家新式戏院，因此轰动京城。此后，开设在珠市口西大街的"第一舞台"模仿上海大舞台，一改往日戏园长条板凳看戏的习惯，建立三层观众厅，二层设置包厢，整个剧场能容纳三千人。而位于珠市口一带的文明戏园，则是京师首开夜场戏的戏园子，并且接待女性进园看戏，还开创了女伶登台表演的先例。

各具特色的宗教建筑

MULTIRELIGIOUS SACRED ARCHITECTURE

Being a city of more than 3,000 years old and with a capital history of over 800 years, Beijing can be seen as a melting pot of the long-standing historical inheritance of various ethnic groups in China, forming a diversified and integrated religious culture. Buddhism, Taoism, Islam, Christianity, and other religions all enjoyed their own development in Beijing and left the city with a variety of religious structures.

有着三千余年建城史、八百余年建都史的北京，汇聚了华夏各民族悠久的历史传承，形成了多元融合的宗教文化。佛教、道教、伊斯兰教、基督教等宗教文化在北京经历了各具特色的发展过程，也在北京城内留下了风格多样的宗教建筑。

The White Stupa Temple

The White Stupa Temple, or Miaoying Temple of the Ming Dynasty, was home to the oldest and largest Tibetan-style white pagoda of the Yuan Dynasty in Beijing. While the temple was built in 1271, the eighth year of the Yuan emperor Zhiyuan's reign, the White Stupa was designed by the Nepalese artisan Araniko. This was quite a huge temple where lots of important Buddhist events were held during the Yuan Dynasty. There used to be a hall inside showcasing the bust of Kublai Khan.

白塔寺

白塔寺，原名大圣寿万安寺，到明代改名妙应寺。寺内所建佛塔是北京地区现存最早、规模最大的元代藏式佛塔。该寺始建于元朝至元八年（1271），佛塔系由尼泊尔著名工匠阿尼哥所建。该寺的规模十分宏大，寺中曾设有元世祖的御容殿。元朝许多重要的佛事皆在此举行。

Dongyue Temple

Dongyue Temple located east of Chaoyangmen Gate was a famous shrine belonging to the Zhengyi sect Taoism which pays tribute to the God of Mount Tai (a.k.a. Dongyue, the eastern peak of the Five Mountains of China). The God of Mount Tai has been one of the main deities worshipped by Taoism, so there are many temples of the same name around China. The Dongyue Temple in Beijing was built in the Yuan Dynasty, and there used to be statues of the 72 Officers of Hell inside to exhort visitors to show mercy instead of to be evil. Those statues were destroyed many years ago; what we see today are replicas. A couple of impersonated imps were said to be standing in front of the entrance to the temple as well, greeting every visitor by the same words: "Here you are, finally!"

东岳庙

东岳庙位于朝阳门外，是道教正一派的著名道观。东岳大帝是道教供奉的主要神灵之一，故而全国各地设置有许多东岳庙，而东岳崇拜也在民间有广泛影响。这座东岳庙始建于元代，观中曾设有地狱七十二司的塑像，让参观者趋善避恶。塑像在多年前被毁，今日所见为后人重塑。

相传清末民初东岳庙会在门口安排两人扮作地府门口小鬼，向前来参观的游客说："你可来了。"

161

Tianning Temple

Tianning Temple, located to the northwest of Guang'anmen Gate, was originally built in the late 5th century during the reign of emperor Xiaowen of Northern Wei. Being one of the oldest temples in Beijing, the pagoda behind it dates back to the Liao Dynasty. In the Qing Dynasty, the temple was famous for its flower fairs, especially of osmanthus and autumn chrysanthemum. Every spring and autumn, local literati and poets went on a wine-tasting outing there to enjoy the blossoms which inspired their poems.

天宁寺

天宁寺位于北京广安门外北面，据称始建于5世纪末北魏孝文帝时，是北京地区最古老的寺庙之一。辽代曾在寺后建舍利塔一座，即现存的"天宁寺塔"。到了清代，天宁寺中"设有花肆，尤以桂花、秋菊为有名"，每到春秋两季京城中人纷纷携酒前去吟诗赏花，留下不少诗篇。

Baiyunguan (The White Cloud Taoist Temple)

Located northwest of Xibianmen Gate, the White Cloud Taoist Temple was one of the three places of origin of Quanzhen (the Complete Perfection) Taoism, and the premier of them all. Built in the Yuan Dynasty, it was the site where Qiu Chuji was believed to become an immortal. Emperor Kangxi of the Qing Dynasty had received instruction here too when he was still a prince. The pair of musical instruments, a gold clapperless bell and a jade chime used in Taoist ceremonies, were well preserved by the temple as it was a gift from Kangxi when he converted to Taoism there.

白云观

白云观位于北京西便门外，是道教全真三大祖庭之一，有"道教全真第一丛林"之称，始建于元代，是全真派祖师丘处机羽化成仙之地。康熙皇帝还是太子的时候也来这里受戒，现存于白云观的金钟玉磬就是康熙受戒时所赐之物。

Fayuan Temple (The Temple of the Origin of the Dharma)

Located to the south of Caishikou, Fayuan Temple, named Minzhong Temple in the first place, was built in the Tang Dynasty and is well over 1,300 years old. Emperor Yongzheng of the Qing Dynasty held the belief that the Vinaya school was the scholastic tradition of Buddhism, so he renamed it the Temple of the Origin of the Dharma. Despite numerous reconstructions since the Tang Dynasty, the temple is still where it was providing a lens to identify the location of the ancient town of Youzhou (an old name for Beijing in the Tang Dynasty). One celebrated visit there was made by Rabindranath Tagore in April, 1924. Accompanied by Xu Zhimo, the Indian poet appreciated the lilac-bloomed Fayuan Temple.

法源寺

法源寺位于菜市口南面，建于唐代，距今已有1300多年的历史。该寺原称悯忠寺，到清代，雍正帝认为佛法之源始于律宗，遂将其改名为法源寺。自唐代以来，法源寺虽经重修，但寺址始终未变，为印证唐幽州城址提供了重要依据。1924年4月，印度诗人泰戈尔在徐志摩陪同下前来观赏寺中丁香，曾留下一段中外文人交往的佳话。

The Yellow Temple

The Yellow Temple was located to the north of Andingmen Gate. At first, there was a pair of them, but the East Yellow Temple built during the Qing emperor Shunzhi's reign no longer existed. The West Yellow Temple was built in the first year of emperor Yongzheng's reign in 1723 and rebuilt by his son Qianlong, specially reserved for the 6th Panchen Lama's visit to the capital for Qianlong's birthday. A cenotaph was ordained by Qianlong in memorial of this very Panchen Lama who later passed away in Beijing.

黄寺

黄寺在安定门外，原分为东黄寺与西黄寺。东黄寺为顺治年间所建，现已不存，西黄寺则是雍正元年（1723）所建，乾隆年间重修，并作为当时西藏宗教领袖六世班禅进京祝寿的驻锡之地。及至六世班禅在京病逝，乾隆帝又为他在这里建了衣冠塔，称清净化城之塔。

雍和宫

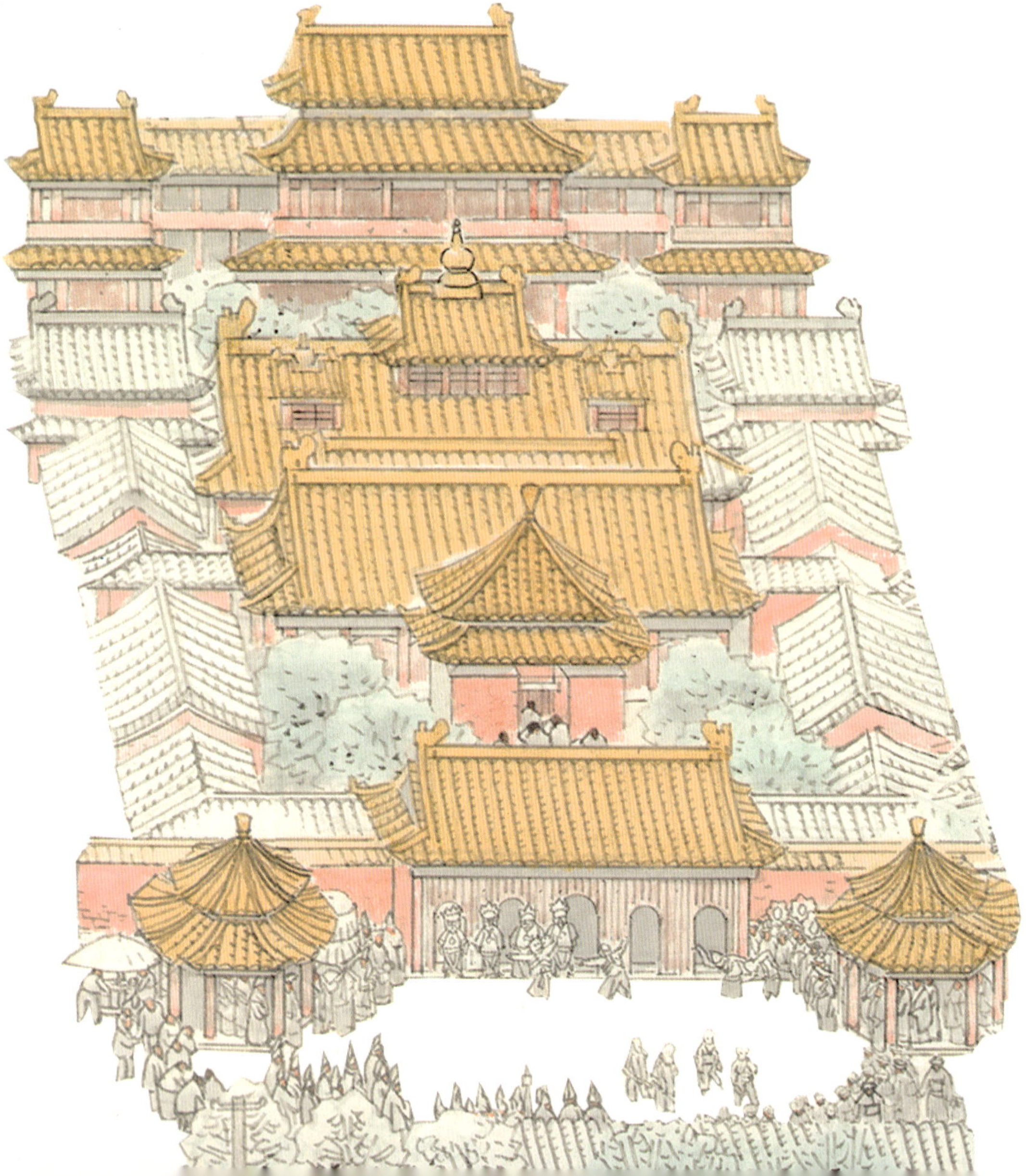

Yonghe Palace (The Lama Temple)

The Lama Temple is located south of Andingmen Gate in Dongcheng district. First constructed in 1694, the thirty-third year of the Qing emperor Kangxi's reign, it was once a residence for his successor Prince Yongzheng. After Yongzheng ascended the throne, he renamed it the Lama Temple. After his death, the Lama Temple was turned into a Tibetan Buddhist Temple by emperor Qianlong. It has been under official protection since 1949, and was listed as a major historical and cultural site protected at the national level in 1961.

雍和宫

雍和宫位于安定门内，初建于清康熙三十三年（1694），是雍正帝即位前居住的王府，在他即位后改为雍和宫。雍正帝去世后，乾隆帝将其改为藏传佛教寺院，仍称雍和宫。新中国成立后，雍和宫受到保护。1961年，雍和宫被列为全国重点文物保护单位。

Niujie Mosque

Located in Niujie Street east of Guang'anmen Gate, Niujie Mosque was among the biggest and oldest mosques in Beijing, and the first in rank when the four grand official temples of the Ming Dynasty are concerned. Viewed from the outside, this palatial architecture is in traditional Chinese design, while its interior decoration manifests Arabic influences, embodying a unique blend of the Chinese and Islamic architectural styles. The mosque was twice renovated after 1949, and listed as a major historical and cultural site protected at the national level in 1988.

牛街清真寺

牛街清真寺位于广安门内牛街，是北京地区规模最大、历史最久的清真寺之一，在明代被称为"四大官寺"之首。该清真寺为中国宫殿式建筑，内部装修结合阿拉伯式建筑风格，形成了中国伊斯兰教建筑的独特形式。新中国成立后，这里曾得到两次大规模修缮，1988年被列为全国重点文物保护单位。

Xuanwumen Church (The Cathedral of the Immaculate Conception)

The Cathedral of the Immaculate Conception, colloquially known as the South Church or Xuanwumen Church to the locals, was the earliest Roman Catholic church in Beijing. In 1605, the thirty-third year of the Ming emperor Wanli's reign, Jesuit Matteo Ricci (Chinese name Li Madou) established a chapel near Xuanwumen Gate. Housed in its affiliated library were Western astronomical instruments, globes, and so on. During the early Qing Dynasty, Jesuit Johann Adam Schall von Bell expanded the chapel into a cathedral equipped with an observatory, a chamber for astronoical instruments, and a library. This was the window through which the Western missionaries evangelized and the Chinese people gained access to Western sciences.

宣武门教堂

宣武门教堂又称南堂,是北京历史最为悠久的天主教教堂。明万历三十三年(1605),神父利玛窦在宣武门内建立第一座经堂并开办图书馆,展示西方天文仪器、地球仪等。清代初年,传教士汤若望在此基础上又建造了一座教堂,教堂内有天文台、仪器馆、藏书楼等,是西方传教士传播天主教的主要场所,也是当时中国人接触西方科学的一个窗口。

Xishiku Cathedral (The Church of the Savior)

The Church of the Savior is also known as Beitang (North Church) or Xishiku Cathedral. It was built on a bestowed by the Qing emperor Kangxi on two French Jesuits who healed him from illness. During emperor Guangxu's reign, the church was moved from its original site at Canchikou to Xishiku. Like square pegs in round holes, there were Chinese stone lions and imperial steles in front of this Gothic-style architecture, a scene hardly to be found in Beijing.

西什库教堂

西什库教堂又称北堂，是法国传教士在治愈康熙帝疾病而获得赐地后，建立起的一座天主教教堂。光绪年间，清朝统治者命令将教堂由蚕池口原址迁至西什库新址。该教堂是哥特式建筑，却配以中国式石狮和谕旨碑亭，是北京城里不多见的西洋建筑。

171

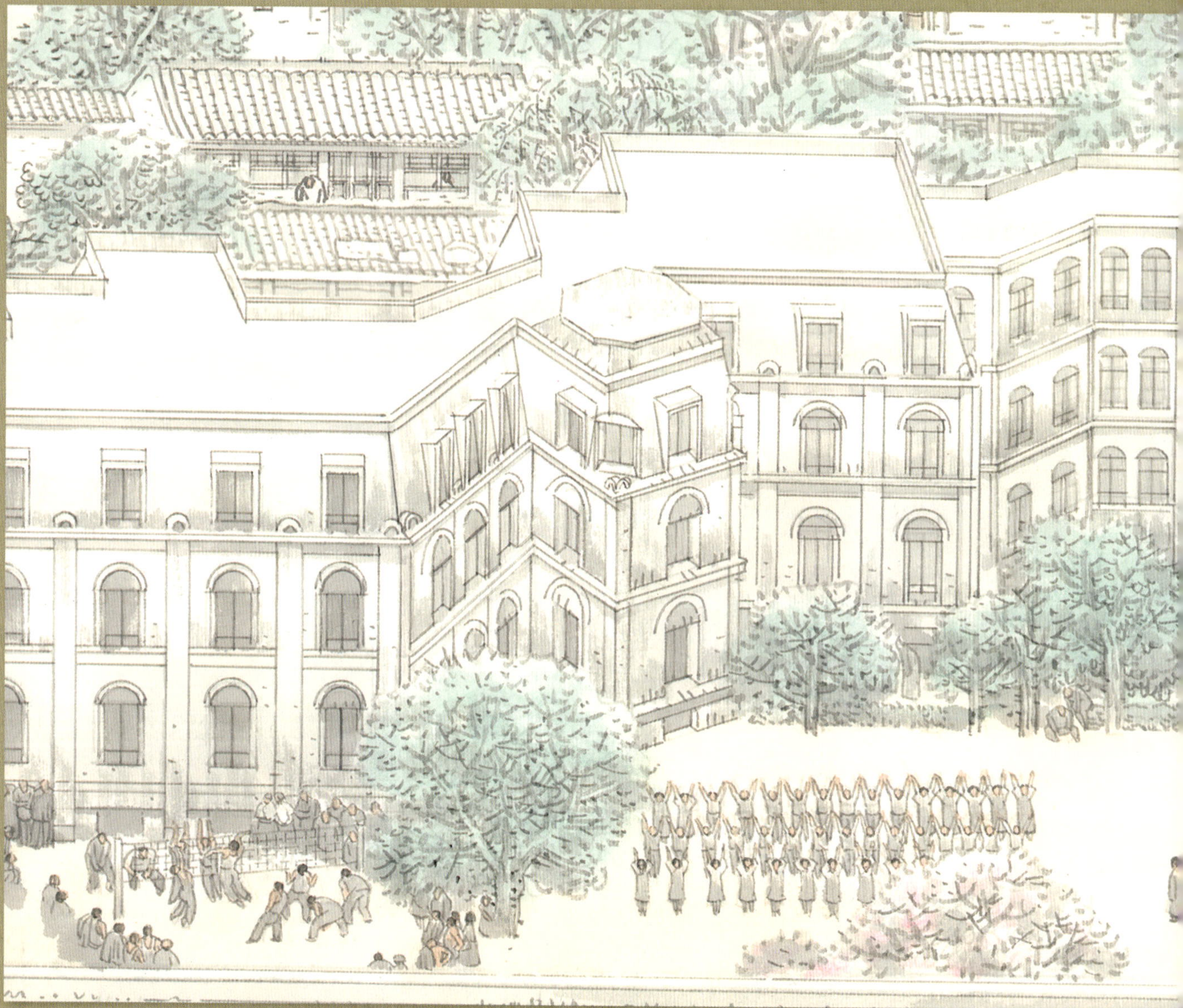

第四章 新文化传播
CHAPTER 4 SPREAD OF NEW IDEAS

In ancient China, politics and culture were closely related. By being the capital of the nation, Beijing naturally functioned as the cultural center. Greatly impacted by Western cultures during the late Qing Dynasty, such a city with profound cultural foundation and long cultural tradition was also influenced by new ideological trends.

As the times required, China's modern educational system emerged from its predecessor which centered on the imperial college examinations. Modern higher education which started from the late Qing reforms remained prosperous even after the founding of the Republic of China. Following the pattern of Peking University, clusters of modern universities were set up, turning Beijing into a national center of higher education. As the major participants of China's modern education, college teachers and students with new thoughts played a vanguard role in the social transformation.

The strong ideological and cultural atmosphere also gave birth to a large number of news agencies and publishing organizations, consequently changing the mindset of the masses as well as their political consciousness. Those newly established social groups and political parties were in the public eye through giving speeches or gathering in public spaces such as parks and guild halls. What they appealed to was widely propagated, propelling the ideological trends exerting influences on Beijing's political situation. As the former imperial capital, every move that Beijing made would be followed by powerful demonstrations and imitation effects for other parts of the country.

在中国古代，政治与文化往往有着非常紧密的关联。数百年来，北京以其都城的政治地位，一直是全国的文化中心。清末西方文化的影响越来越大，给有着深厚文化基础、悠久文化传统的北京，带来了新思潮的涌动。

近代新式教育从以国子监、太学为中心的教育体制中应运而生。由清末新政开启的近代高等教育在民国建立后得到繁荣发展，在北京大学的示范作用下，一批近代大学相继成立，北京成为国家高等教育中心。带有新思想的老师和学生成为新式教育的主体，并且在社会变革的大潮中成为先锋。

浓厚的新式思想文化氛围催生了一批新闻出版机构，在它们的鼓呼下，众多市民的思想观念和政治意识开始发生转变。新的社会团体和政党在公园、会馆等公共空间进行演讲或集会，他们的诉求和主张通过传媒形成新的思潮，影响着北京政治风云的变幻。作为帝都，北京的一举一动在全国都有着巨大的示范与传导作用。

面向西方的教育转型
WESTERNIZED EDUCATIONAL TRANSFORMATION

Confucius Temple & Guozijian (The Imperial College)

  The Confucius Temple and the Imperial College (Guozijian, literally meaning School for the Sons of the State in Chinese) are standing next to each other south of Andingmen Gate. The architectural layout of having the Imperial College on the west and Confucius Temple on the east is in line with the tradition in ancient China. Confucius Temple was the imperial venue where emperors of the Yuan, Ming, and Qing dynasties held worshipping ceremonies for Confucius to spread his teachings and manifest their respect and advocation for the Confucian culture. The Imperial College, on the other hand, was the highest national institution of higher learning ever since the Yuan and into the Qing dynasties. Through formal schooling and the imperial examination, a large number of graduates from there became qualified personnels for the governing of the state. After the abolition of the imperial examination, the Imperial College ceased to function as an educational institution.

孔庙与国子监

　　孔庙与国子监位于安定门内,呈东西并排分布,国子监在西侧,孔庙在东侧,体现了中国古代"庙学并列"的传统。孔庙是皇帝祭祀孔子的场所,是元明清三代皇帝尊崇孔子、倡兴文教之地。国子监则是元明清三代的全国最高学府和教育管理机构,通过教育和科举考试,为国家输送了大量治国理政的人才。清末科举制度废除后,国子监的教育职能也随即废止。

The Imperial Examination Center

The Imperial Examination Center in Beijing was used as a venue for imperial examinations at various levels during the Ming and Qing dynasties, serving mostly township examinees from Shuntianfu, or high-ranking township examinees from different provinces. The center had booths for examinees to answer questions and watchtowers at the four corners of the compound for invigilation purposes. Following the abolition of the imperial examination in 1905, the place was gradually taken up by residential dwellings. It is now the location of the Chinese Academy of Social Sciences.

贡院

　　北京的贡院是明清两代举行科举考试的考场，通常举行的是顺天府乡试和全国会试。北京贡院内设有供考生应试的考棚，贡院四角还设有瞭望楼，用于监考。1905年科举被废除后，这里也逐渐变为民居，现被改建为中国社会科学院。

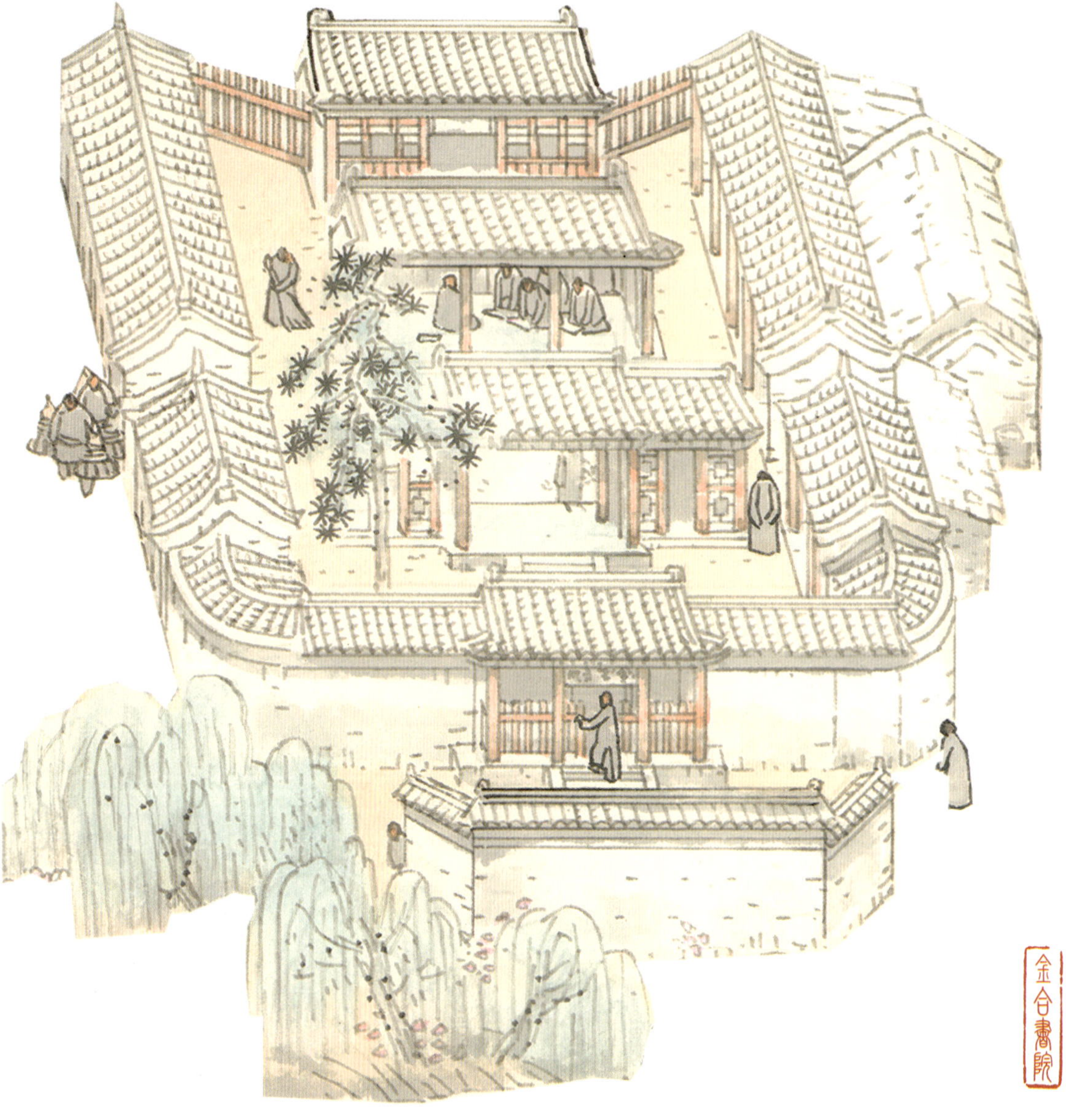
金台書院

Jintai Academy

Academies (*shuyuan*) were educational institutions presided over by scholars in feudal China. Jintai Academy was established in the Qing Dynasty and is the most typical and well-preserved of its kind in Beijing. Once upon a time in this part of the city, there used to be a scenic spot included in the Eight Sights of Yanjing. The scene was depicted as Evening Glow on Golden Terrace. The academy was named after that. Following the abolition of the imperial examination system, Jintai Academy was changed into a popular school called Shunzhi, recruiting students in the surrounding densely populated, impoverished areas like Longxugou and Jinyuchi(Gold Fish Pond). The site is today's Jintai Academy Primary School of Beijing's Dongcheng district.

金台书院

书院，是中国古代由学者主持的教育机构。金台书院建立于清代，是北京历史上保存下来的最经典、最完整的书院。该书院取"燕京八景"之一的"金台夕照"命名。科举废除后，金台书院改为顺直学堂，曾面向周边龙须沟、金鱼池等贫民聚居区，广招贫困学童，深得人心。金台书院现为东城区金台书院小学。

Peking University

Peking University, formerly known as the Imperial University of Peking, was established in 1898. It was the first national comprehensive university and the start of modern education in China. In 1917, Cai Yuanpei became the principal of Peking University. His philosophy on running the university was "freedom of thought and embracement of diversity", which attracted a bunch of influential scholars to lecture there. In 1918, the Red Building, a landmark building on campus, was completed. Chen Duxiu, a key founding member of the Communist Party of China, was also a teacher at Peking University. With his avant-garde magazine *La Jeunesse*, Chen exalted democracy and science, supported the rising New Culture Movement, and eventually became a vital force in the upcoming May Fourth Movement. In 1920, Li Dazhao, a pioneer of the Chinese Communist movement, established the Beijing Communist Group at the Red Building, a de facto base for the dissemination of Marxism.

Scan QR code for VR experience

北京大学

扫码观看现在的北大红楼

　　北京大学的前身是京师大学堂，创建于1898年，是中国第一所国立综合性大学，开启了中国近代教育的先河。1917年，蔡元培出任北京大学校长，实行"思想自由，兼容并包"的办学方针，招收了一批有巨大社会影响力的著名学者到此任教。1918年，北大标志性建筑红楼落成，中共主要创始人之一陈独秀曾执教北大，并以《新青年》杂志为核心，宣传民主与科学思想，推动新文化运动的蓬勃发展，为五四运动的爆发积蓄了力量。1920年，中国共产主义运动先驱李大钊在红楼建立北京共产主义小组，红楼也成了马克思主义的宣传阵地。

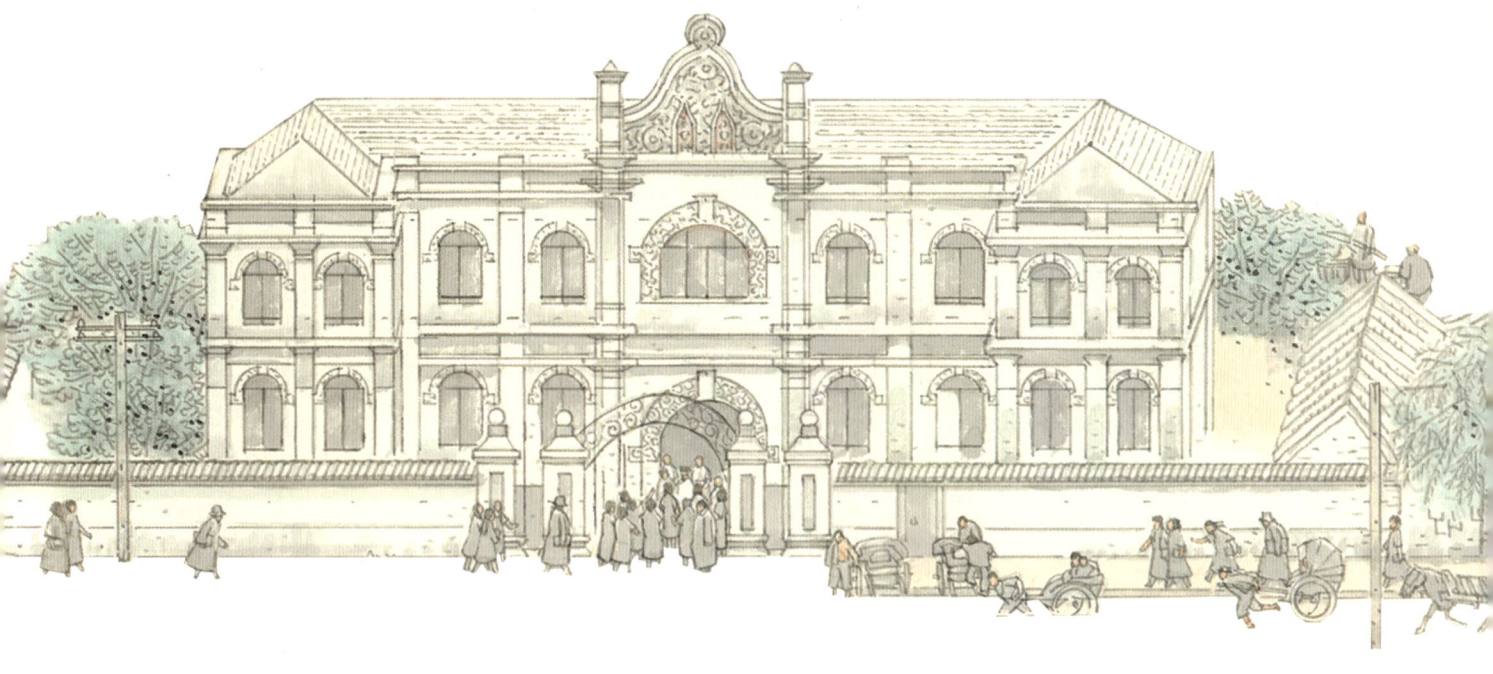

Peking Female Normal School

The Imperial Female Normal School was built in 1908 by the Qing authority and renamed Peking Female Normal School in 1912. Located north of the Xuanwumen Gate, it was the first national higher education institution for women in China. During the early years of the Republic of China, it was the center of higher education for Chinese women, with nearly one-third of the country's women students received higher education there before they grew into qualified talents in society. Among those who had taught there were bigwigs such as Li Dazhao and Lu Xun. The premises of the former college is now the Beijing Luxun High School.

北京女子师范学校

北京女子师范大学的前身是京师女子师范学堂，1908年由清政府创办，1912年更名为北京女子师范学校。该校位于宣武门内，是中国第一所国立女子高等学府。民国初年，这所学校是中国女性接受高等教育的中心，国内近1/3接受高等教育的女性就读于该校，为社会培养了大量女性人才。李大钊、鲁迅等著名学者皆曾在此任教。该校现为北京市鲁迅中学。

Peking Academy

Peking Academy was first founded in 1871, the tenth year of the Qing emperor Tongzhi's reign. Located northeast of Chongwenmen Gate, it was once a kindergarten affiliated to the Methodist Episcopal Church. In 1888, it became Peking Academy(*Shuyuan*), offering disciplines in liberal arts, science, theology, medicine, and art. From 1912 on, it was called Peking College. In 1918, after merging with the North China Union College in today's Tongzhou district and the North China Union College for Women to form Yenching University, the higher education section of the Peking College relocated to the premises of Peking University in today's Haidian district. The remaining preparatory school and secondary school formed the new Peking Academy. Both the calligraphic name on the badge and the motto of the academy were dedicated by Cai Yuanpei, highlighting its eminent status in the history of modern private schools in Beijing.

汇文学校

汇文学校成立于清同治十年（1871），位于崇文门内路东，其前身是美国基督教会美以美会附设的蒙学馆，1888年更名为"汇文书院"，增设大学部，开设文、理、神、医、艺术等科目。1912年更名为"汇文大学校"。1918年，汇文大学校大学部与通州协和大学、华北协和女子大学合并为"燕京大学"，迁至海淀区今北京大学校址。原校址留下大学预科和中学两部，定名为"汇文学校"，由蔡元培先生亲自题写校名和校训。汇文学校是北京近代私立学校的代表。

The Press and Publishing

Towards the late Qing Dynasty and the beginning of the Republic of China, Beijing was rolled in by not only a large number of opinion leaders in politics and culture, but also masses of college students awakened by the New Culture Movement. The city back then was surrounded by a strong political atmosphere as well as heated cultural debates on public opinions shaped by several leading newspapers and periodicals. With its editorial office based in Peking University, *La Jeunesse* played a key role in the New Culture Movement in which the ideas of democracy and science were propagated. *Morning Post* and its supplements enjoyed a wide readership among the public, with Li Dazhao being the first editor-in-chief, while Lu Xun and Xu Zhimo being the contributing writers. Run by Shao Piaoping, a newspaper industry insider, the *Jingbao* (*Peking Gazette*) was a popular public magazine dedicated to speaking for the people.

报馆

清末民初，北京汇集了大批政界、文化界名流，还有许多受到新文化运动洗礼的高校学子，政治氛围浓厚，文化讨论热烈，引领社会风潮的著名报刊则构建起自己的舆论阵地。《新青年》以北京大学为阵地，发起新文化运动，宣传民主与科学的思想；《晨报》及其副刊曾由李大钊任第一任总编，鲁迅、徐志摩等著名学者都曾为其主笔，极具社会影响力；报人邵飘萍创办的《京报》则因定位在为民众发表意见的媒介而广受好评。

187

Taoran Pavilion (Joyous Pavilion) and Cibe Temple (The Temple of Mercy)

Situated in the southern part of Beijing, the Taoran Pavilion was a gathering site frequented by literati during the Qing Dynasty. The Pavilion was close to the ancient Temple of Mercy. Since modern times, visits by patriots have ranged from Lin Zexu (who spared no effort to rid China of opium at Humen) to Kang Youwei and Liang Qichao (the Hundred Days reformers), and from Qiu Jin (a martyr of the Revolution of 1911) to Sun Yat-sen (the founding father of the Republic of China). Circa 1920, Mao Zedong and Zhou Enlai met with like-minded friends there respectively, drawing up future blueprints for China.

Scan QR code for VR experience

陶然亭 – 慈悲庵

　　陶然亭位于北京城南,清代成为文人墨客的雅集之地。许多诗篇从这里流传,这里许多文人的聚会也备受后人推崇。陶然亭旁的古刹慈悲庵,更是近代以来爱国志士的集会之地。从销毁鸦片的林则徐到戊戌变法时期的康有为、梁启超,再到辛亥革命时的秋瑾、民国初年的孙中山等,都曾在慈悲庵留下足迹。1920 年,毛泽东与周恩来也均来到此地集会,为当时中国的未来描绘远景。

扫码观看现在的陶然亭

南城会馆

会馆是明清两代为解决各地商贾经商、举子赶考而在京设置的场馆。这些会馆平常的公共活动就较多，及至科举考试制度被废除后，会馆更是成为举办各类社会活动的公共场所，很多进步活动都是在城南的会馆中进行的。1912年8月，孙中山出席在湖广会馆举行的同盟会会员欢迎大会；陈独秀在南城办报时曾长期居住在安庆会馆；鲁迅也在日记中记载过他去安庆会馆参加活动时的情景。

Guild Halls

Guild halls were mainly for the accommodations of businessmen or examinees who came to the capital for trade or the imperial examinations from the same township as the guild leader during the Ming and Qing dynasties. After the abolition of the imperial examination, social activities of different kinds were even more flourishing at guild halls in the southern part of Beijing. Among them, there were many progressive activities. In August, 1912, Sun Yat-sen attended a welcoming ceremony held at the Huguang Guild Hall for members of Tongmenghui (the Chinese Revolutionary League). When Chen Duxiu ran a newspaper with his editorial office in this neighborhood, he had a long stay at the Anqing Guild Hall, a place which was also mentioned in Lu Xun's diary as being the venue for an event.

湖广会馆
Huguang Guild Hall

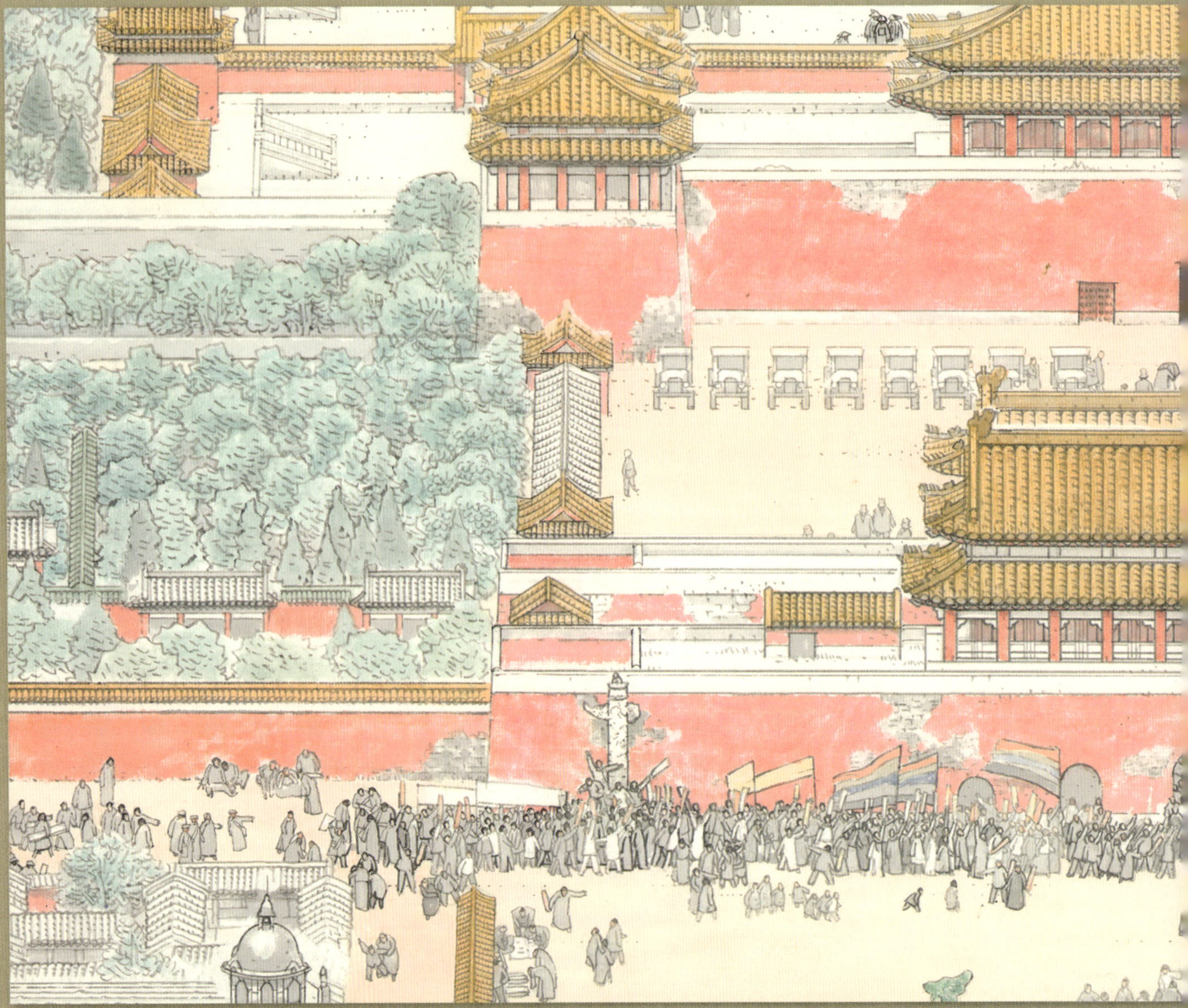

第五章 时局与事件

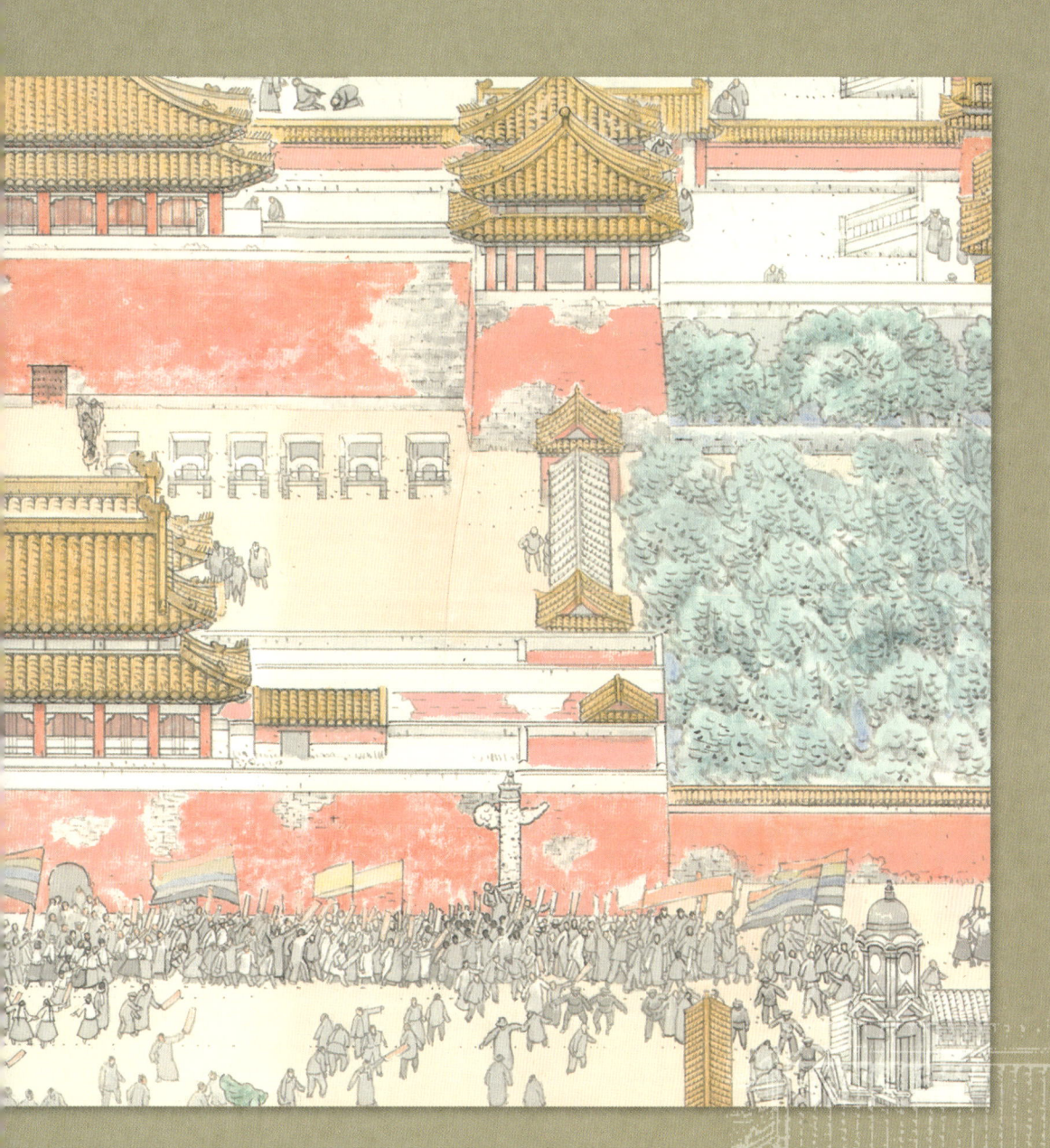

CHAPTER 5 POLITICAL SITUATION AND LANDMARK EVENTS

The 1910s was a decade dominated by political turmoil in the history of modern China. The Revolution of 1911 put an end to the 2,000-year-long monarchy in China, and ushered in a republic form of government. The change of government gave rise to the flexing of muscles by various parties. As a political center through the Chinese history, Beijing has been a mirror of the nation's political situation.

Far-reaching historical events took their turns happening in the city: shifting the capital of the provisional republic government from Nanjing to Beijing, coercing Congress into electing Yuan Shikai to the presidency, Yuan proclaiming himself the Hongxian emperor, and Puyi being restored to the throne by Zhang Xun. Similar incidents in other parts of the country included the Second Revolution in 1913, the National Protection War from 1915 to 1916, and the Movement to Protect the Constitution in 1917. The underlying causes of all these were the rise and fall of social forces among the holdovers from the Qing Dynasty, the Beiyang warlords, and the political party of the bourgeois. A outwardly unified China was indeed being torn apart.

Amid the political and civil strife, one new force emerged. Chen Duxiu, Li Dazhao, Hu Shi, and other advanced intellectuals launched the New Culture Movement by championing democracy and science. With the salvoes of Russia's October Revolution in 1917, Marxism-Leninism was introduced to China, bringing the New Culture Movement to the next phrase. At the news of China's diplomatic failure at the Paris Peace Conference, Chinese youths influenced by the new ideas took to the streets and chanted slogans reading: "Defend our sovereignty from external force, and get rid of traitors in our country!" It was in Beijing that the May Fourth Movement erupted into a nationwide champaign later on.

Soon after in 1921, the founding of the Communist Party of China ushered in a new era for the country.

1910—1920年是中国近代史上政治局势极为动荡的十年。辛亥革命后，延续了两千年的帝制宣告终结，共和政体得以确立。新旧政权交替之际，各方势力暗流涌动。北京，这个历来的政治中心，依然引领着全国局势的走向。

临时政府北迁、国会风波、袁世凯恢复帝制、张勋复辟等重大历史事件在北京城接连上演，二次革命、护国运动、护法运动等事件也在各地持续爆发。这些事件表明：清朝遗老、北洋军阀、资产阶级政党等几种社会势力的激烈斗争此消彼长，表面上的统一掩盖不住实质上的分裂。

在各种政治力量相互角逐之时，一种新的力量勃然兴起。陈独秀、李大钊、胡适等先进知识分子高举"民主"与"科学"两面大旗，发起了新文化运动。十月革命一声炮响，给中国送来了马克思主义，使新文化运动有了进一步发展的方向。当巴黎和会中国政府外交失败的消息传回国内，受新思潮影响的民众走上街头，发出"外争主权，内除国贼"的呐喊，五四运动的影响由北京辐射全国。

1921年，中国共产党成立，中国进入了一个全新的时代。

THE ABDICATION OF THE QING EMPEROR

清帝退位

The Revolution of 1911 overthrew the Qing Dynasty. On January 1, 1912, Sun Yat-sen was elected the Provisional President of the Republic of China in Nanjing. Through the mediation of Yuan Shikai, the Empress Dowager Longyu agreed to sign an abdication of the Xuantong emperor on February 12, on the condition that the imperial family would keep its extravagant lifestyles with the living expenses being paid by the government of the Republic of China. It put an end to the 2,000-year-long monarchy in China. After the abdication, Puyi continued living in the Forbidden City, only without the freedom to exit. To ease himself from the crave for the world outside, he often climbed up the roof of a palace hall within the Forbidden City to look off into the distance.

1911年的辛亥革命掀起推翻清朝统治的巨浪。1912年1月1日，孙中山在南京宣誓就任中华民国临时大总统，推行共和政体。1912年2月12日，在袁世凯的斡旋下，隆裕太后以宣统皇帝的名义接受南京临时政府的优待条件，颁布了《退位诏书》，结束了延续两千余年的帝制。溥仪退位之后，仍然生活在紫禁城内，生活费用由民国政府拨给，过着优裕的生活，但不能自由出入。为了能看到外面的世界，他爬上宫殿的顶部，眺望远方。

197

北洋兵变
THE MUTINY STAGED BY BEIYANG WARLORDS

After the abdication of the Qing emperor, Sun Yat-sen ceded his position as the Provisional President of the Republic of China to Yuan Shikai but required the latter to take office in Nanjing. In order to stay within his sphere of influence, Yuan had his men stage a camouflaged mutiny on the night of February 29, 1912, marking widespread turmoil in Beijing as well as nearby Baoding and Tianjin, and creating the illusion of an unstable political situation in northern China. He was backed by Beiyang warlords such as Duan Qirui and Feng Guozhang, all in favor of establishing a provisional authority in Beijing. Meanwhile, Yuan received open support from foreign countries who refused to recognize the Nanjing authority as a diplomatic gesture. Finally, the Provisional Senate in Nanjing agreed to let Yuan take office in Beijing.

清帝退位后，孙中山按约定将中华民国临时大总统一职让位于袁世凯，但要求袁世凯必须到南京就职。为了留在自己的势力范围内，1912年2月29日夜，袁世凯指使手下伪装兵变，在北京城内闹事、抢掠，事件波及保定、天津一带，营造出北方政局不稳定的假象。段祺瑞、冯国璋等北洋将领也要求必须在北京建立临时政府，西方各国同时公开支持袁世凯上台，对南京临时政府不予外交承认。最终，临时参议院同意袁世凯在北京就职。

北洋新军检阅
Beiyang troops on parade

袁世凯就任临时大总统
YUAN SHIKAI ASSUMED PRESIDENCY OF THE REPUBLIC OF CHINA

On March 10, 1912, Yuan Shikai was sworn in as the Provisional President. He nominated heads of Beiyang warlords as ministers of foreign affairs, the army, and internal affairs, and revolutionary and reformist figures as ministers of education, justice, and agriculture, industry, and commerce. On April 1, the ministers took office in Beijing. Four days later, members of the Provisional House and Senate arrived in Beijing to prepare for a formal Congress. Many newly founded political parties moved their headquarters from southern China to Beijing, too, enlivening the city's political atmosphere.

袁世凯在居仁堂
Yuan Shikai at Jurentang Hall

1912年3月10日，袁世凯就任临时大总统，提名北洋派首脑出任外交、陆军、内务等部总长，革命党和改良派人物则出任教育、司法、农工商等部总长，4月1日到北京就职。4月5日，临时国会参众两会议员来到北京，筹办正式国会。许多南方新生政党也把总部迁到北京，活跃了北京的政治气氛。

THE MEETINGS BETWEEN SUN YAT-SEN AND YUAN SHIKAI IN BEIJING

孙中山与袁世凯北京会面

On August 24, 1912, Sun Yat-sen and his wife visited Beijing at the invitation of Yuan Shikai. Yuan arranged a formal welcome ceremony at Qianmen Railway Station. He presided over a grand welcome banquet at Haiyantang in the Sea Palaces and had Sun accommodated at the office of the Provisional President (the former guesthouse affiliated to the Qing Foreign Ministry) at Shidaren *hutong* near Dongdan.

With the intention of peaceful unification and dissemination of his Principles of People's Livelihood, Sun held secret talks with Yuan for 13 times during his stays in Beijing. Putting faith in Yuan and his faked promises, Sun turned to investing in railways and industries, calling on the whole country to stop the partisanship in the hope of attaining unification between northern and southern China.

1912年8月24日，受袁世凯邀请，孙中山携夫人等来到北京。袁世凯在前门火车站安排了隆重的欢迎仪式，并在中南海海晏堂亲自主持盛大欢迎公宴，又把孙中山安排在东单石大人胡同的临时大总统办公处（原清外务部迎宾馆）居住。在京期间，孙中山抱着和平统一和宣传民生主义的想法，与袁世凯进行了十三次密谈，他轻信了袁世凯的假意附和，自愿投身铁路建设和实业建设，并号召全国停止党派纷争，实现南北统一。

外务部迎宾馆
Guesthouse affiliated to the Qing Foreign Ministry

国会风波
THE TURMOIL IN CONGRESS

On October 6, 1913, the first presidential election of the Republic of China was held at the Congress Hall. In order to secure a victory, Yuan Shikai had the Hall besieged by policemen disguised as citizens, threatening the Members of Congress to vote for him, or they would be prohibited from leaving the venue. After two rounds of voting which lasted till nightfall, Yuan's votes received still fell short of the vote goal. The disguised petitioners rushed into the hall and started to thump the voting members. Under such intimidation, most of the members had to vote for Yuan, who turned out to be the first President of the Republic of China, at the third round of voting.

1913年10月6日,中华民国第一届大总统选举在国会议场举行。为了当选,袁世凯安排军警冒充公民,将国会议场重重包围,要求选举袁为大总统,否则不允许议员走出会场。直到傍晚,经过两轮投票,袁世凯仍未达到法定当选票数。这时"公民团"突然冲进来开始殴打议员。在武力的胁迫下,多数的国会议员在第三轮投票选举袁世凯为中华民国的第一任大总统。

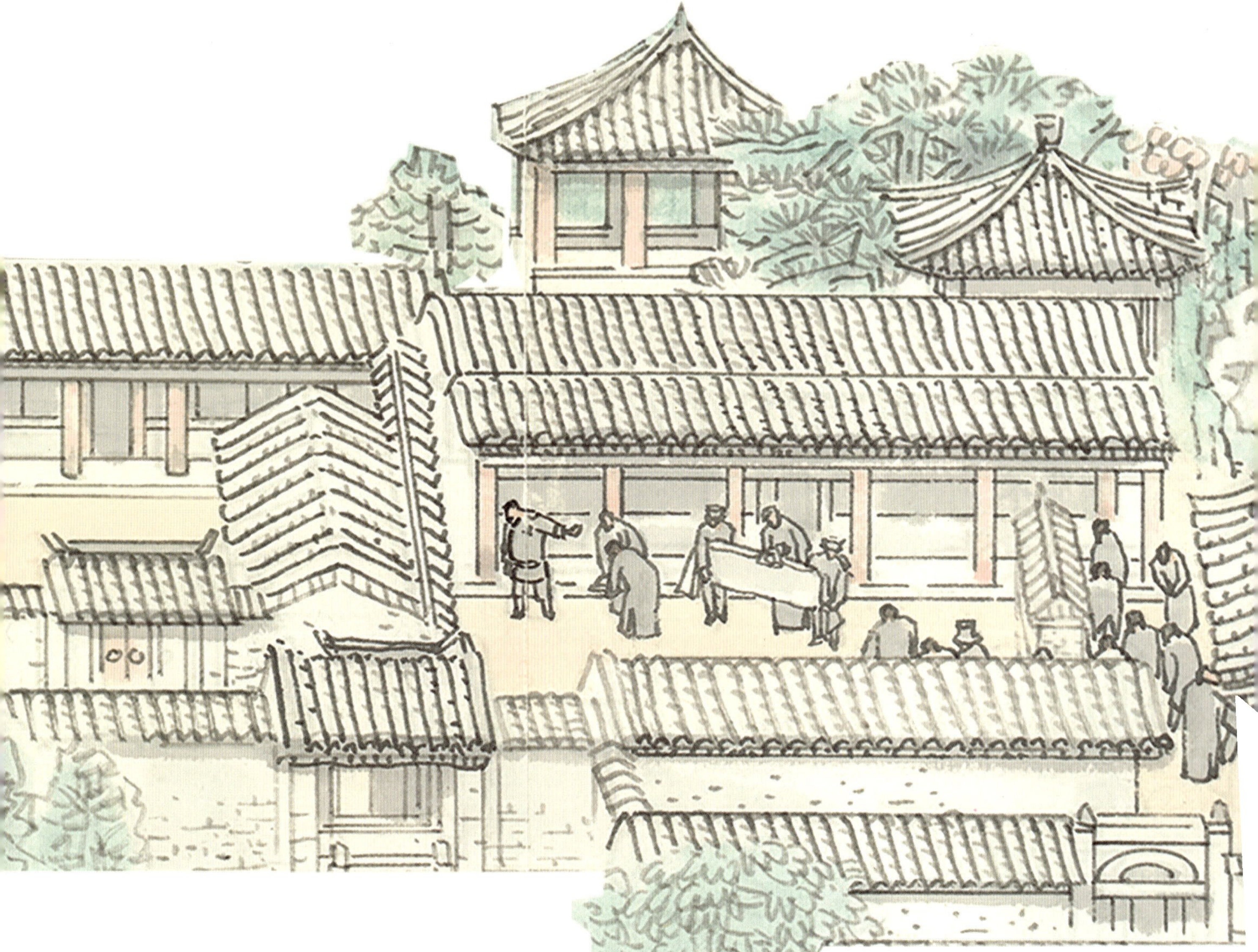

六 黎元洪辞亲王匾
LI YUANHONG'S REFUSAL TO ENDOWMENT

As Yuan Shikai became the President, he got down to the restoration of monarchy. Li Yuanhong, then vice president, was so opposed to this idea that he resigned and moved out of the Sea Palaces to live in Dongchang *hutong*. On December 12, 1915, Yuan proclaimed himself emperor and immediately changed the designation of his reign to Hongxian. He endowed Li as the Prince of the Wuchang Uprising. When Yuan's messenger arrived at Li's with a prince's gown and a plaque personally inscribed by his boss, Li turned them down on the excuse that he did not deserve the honor of a meritorious statesman who led the Revolution of 1911. It literally showcased his opposition to Yuan's claim to the throne.

袁世凯就任总统后便开始筹备复辟帝制，时任副总统黎元洪对此持反对态度，并请辞搬出中南海，迁往东厂胡同居住。1915年12月12日，袁世凯称帝，改元洪宪，颁布的第一道"圣旨"就是册封黎元洪为其建立的中华帝国的"武义亲王"。当袁世凯的使者带着亲王服和袁世凯题写的亲王匾到东厂胡同时，黎元洪以"愧不敢当""辛亥武昌首义之勋"为由，不接受册封，实际表明了自己反对袁世凯称帝的态度。

208

THE DEMOLITION OF THE KETTELER MEMORIAL

The Ketteler Memorial was a marble archway located at Dongdan Beidajie (north street). Clemens August Freiherr von Ketteler, the German ambassador to China, was shot dead by the Qing soldiers in 1900 when he was trying to pick a quarrel. As was stipulated in the *Protocol of 1901*, a monument was required to be erected at Dongdan. The monument stood as an indelible memory of the humiliated past in Chinese history. On November 11, 1918, to celebrate China's victory in World War I, the memorial was demolished by Beijing citizens who had its fragments transported to today's Zhongshan Park where it was reassembled. The inscriptions once thereon were replaced by four Chinese characters. At this point, the Ketteler Memorial was renamed the Archway of Victory of Justice.

克林德碑是位于东单北大街的一座石牌坊。1900年，因清军击毙寻衅滋事的德国外交官克林德，清政府被要求在其遇难处建立纪念碑。这一要求被作为议和条件写入《辛丑条约》，而竖立在东单的克林德碑则成为中国屈辱历史的象征。1918年11月11日，作为第一次世界大战的战胜国，北京市民拆毁克林德碑，并将其散件陆续运至中央公园重新组装，原有文字也被全部清除，改刻为"公理战胜"四个大字，至此，克林德碑改称为"公理战胜牌坊"。

五四运动
THE MAY FOURTH MOVEMENT

The Paris Peace Conference in January, 1919 was participated by the Great Britain, the United States, France, Japan, Italy, and other victorious countries. The Chinese government sent a delegation to Paris to regain Shandong from Germany and Austria. They also wanted to discuss the withdrawal of foreign troops from China, as was granted by the *Protocol of 1901* but were disappointed. Instead, the Allies confirmed Japan's colonial rights and privileges gained in China. The country's diplomatic failure at the conference sparked the far-reaching May Fourth Movement. On the afternoon of May 4, 1919, more than 3,000 students from 13 universities in Beijing gathered in front of Tian'anmen Square, holding banners like "Return Qingdao to China" and "Cancel the Twenty-one Demands", and required those who had engaged in the signing of a traitorous treaty, namely, Cao Rulin, Lu Zongyu, and Zhang Zongxiang, be punished. This major patriotic activity of a nationwide impact was later referred to as the May Fourth Movement.

1919年1月，英、美、法、日、意等战胜国召开巴黎和会，中国作为战胜国参会，要求收回德、奥在华的租借及特权，撤销《辛丑条约》赋予外国在华的驻兵权等，但巴黎和会拒绝中国的要求，并决定由日本继承德国在中国山东的特权。巴黎和会上中国外交的失败，引发了著名的五四运动。1919年5月4日下午，北京十三所高校的三千多名学生代表集结在天安门前，举着"还我青岛""取消二十一条"等标语，要求惩办参与签订卖国条约的曹汝霖、陆宗舆、章宗祥等人。学生们举行了声势浩大的游行，随后在全国产生了广泛影响。这次重大爱国运动，被后人称为五四运动。

火烧赵家楼

THE FIRE ON ZHAOJIALOU LANE

Students of the May Fourth Movement paraded to the mansion of Cao Rulin, the traitor, on Zhaojialou Lane and set it on fire. People from all walks of life showed their support by objecting to the arrest of 32 students, and the May Fourth Movement became a countrywide campaign. On June 5, 1919, industrial workers in Shanghai launched a large-scale strike to express their support for the students, which marked the debut of the working class in modern Chinese history. As a result of increasing pressure from public opinion, Cao Rulin, Lu Zongyu, Zhang Zongxiang, etc., were removed from office, followed by the resignation of President Xu Shichang. The workers' and the students' strikes declined after June 12. Ultimately, the Chinese delegation refused to sign the *Treaty of Versailles* on June 28, 1919.

参加五四运动的学生在示威游行之后，烧掉了卖国贼曹汝霖的住宅赵家楼，随后有三十二名学生被捕。社会各界人士对此给予关注和支持，抗议逮捕学生，五四运动的影响向全国扩散。1919年6月5日，上海工人开始大规模罢工，以响应学生的爱国壮举，工人阶级从此登上历史舞台。面对强大的社会舆论压力，曹、陆、章等人相继被免职，总统徐世昌也提出辞职。1919年6月12日以后，工人相继复工，学生停止罢课。1919年6月28日，中国代表也拒绝在《巴黎和约》上签字。

陈独秀发表《北京市民宣言》
CHEN DUXIU AND HIS MANIFESTO OF THE CITIZENS OF PEKING

On June 11, 1919, Chen Duxiu, then a professor at Peking University, handed out leaflets from the rooftop garden of the New World Shopping Mall and at the Chengnan Amusement Park, announcing the *Manifesto of the Citizens of Peking* he drafted. It presented the Beiyang authority with an ultimatum on behalf of the Beijing citizens on issues including the sovereignty of Shandong province and the autonomy rights of citizens. The Manifesto served as a guideline during the May Fourth Movement. Chen was arrested at the scene, the editorial office of *La Jeunesse* was also closed down.

1919年6月11日，北大教授陈独秀在新世界商场和城南游艺园散发亲自起草的《北京市民宣言》传单。传单代表北京市民就山东主权问题、市民自治问题等对北洋政府提出了最后、最低的要求，是五四运动时期具有指导性意义的宣言。散发传单时，陈独秀遭警察厅逮捕，《新青年》编辑部遭到查封。

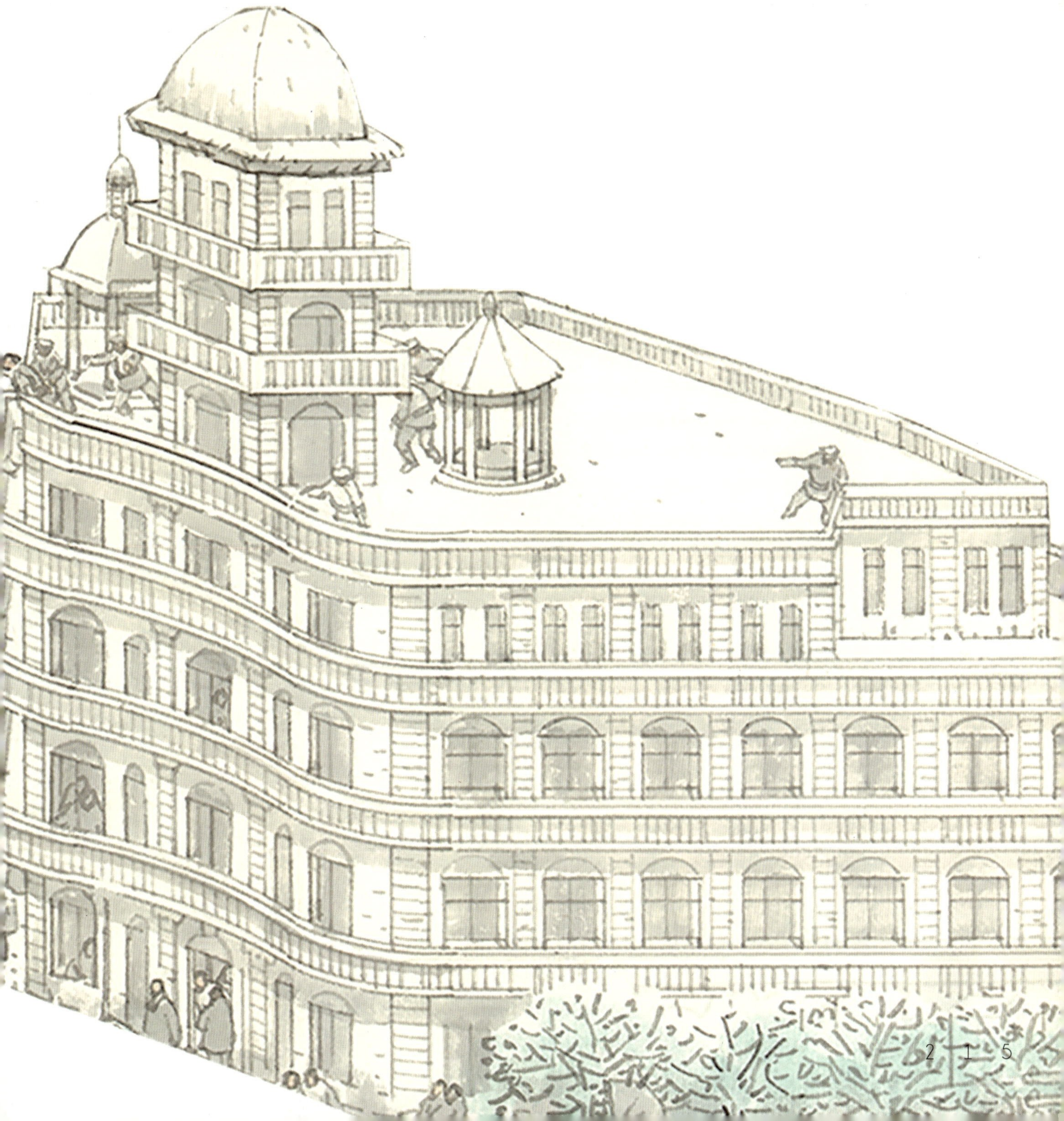

ISBN 978-7-5142-3873-0

定价：138.00 元